BIG IDEAS FOR LITTLE FEET

Deirdre Olliver-Menezes

An Easy-to-read journal
of insightful thoughts

into the world of nurturing children...
from a teacher's
perspective.

With oodles of love,

Periwinkle

Who is this for?

Being a woman, wife, mother, colleague, family member also translates to being a nurse, taxi driver, fairy godmother, genie, super woman, guide, 'head cook and bottle washer'....

All I would want to do is give all of us caregivers a reference point, from a teacher's perspective... to know we are not alone and that there are many of us who are as 'in the dark' as the next person. I am hoping the following pages will be a fresh look at life as we know it. I would not boast to 'know-it all' just to give a little help, a little hope, and oodles of love!

**Warm wishes and hugs,
Periwinkle**

SANATANA DHARMA FOR THE MODERN WORLD

SIMPLIFIED FOR YOU, YOUR TEENAGE KIDS AND YOUR FAMILY

A humble attempt to share
a layman's insights into Hinduism -
The world's oldest, eternal, timeless, and most inclusive religion.

JAYARAM RAJARAM

Dharmo Rakshati Rakshitah (Sanskrit: धर्मो रक्षति रक्षितः)
Dharma Protects Those Who Protect It

"Sanatana Dharma for the Modern World is a book which
I recommend for all ages, especially the young!"
– Sri Dushyanth Sridhar,
Vedic Speaker & Writer,

Foreword by Vedic Scholar Shri Dushyant Sridhar

INDIA · SINGAPORE · MALAYSIA

I pledge to donate 100% of all author earnings after taxes from sale of this book for Dharmic causes only.

– Jayaram Rajaram

Author

FOREWORD

'Bhramara' is a bee. It makes a buzzing sound that excites children. It goes from one flower to another collecting pollen and nectar. The nectar in the bee's stomach becomes honey over a period of time. This honey is stored in the cells of the honeycomb. This honey is then accepted by Paramatma who is found as murtis in various temples.

Similarly, Jayaram has collected the information he has gathered from discourses he has listened to and from reading of books. A good proportion of humility and personal experiences are also mixed in this pudding. The honey that has managed to emerge is this book – 'Sanatana Dharma for the Modern World', which I recommend for all ages, especially the young.

Sri Dushyanth Sridhar
Vedic Speaker & Writer
www.desikadaya.org

ACKNOWLEDGEMENTS

Nothing in this world is possible without the grace of the Almighty. I had not imagined in my wildest dreams that I would be writing a book on our great religion-Sanatana Dharma (Hinduism). Let alone finishing the book, even starting to write a book and the flow of thoughts and learnings along the way is because of the Grace of God and spiritual guidance of my Gurus HH Jagadguru Chandrashekarendra Saraswati Swamigal (Mahaperiyava/ Paramacharya), HH Jagadguru Jayendra Saraswati Swamligal and HH Jagadguru Vijayendra Saraswati Swamigal (Bala Periyava). I know for a fact that my Guru Bala Periyava literally read my mind when I had the thought of writing this book (to help my own family and other Hindus start learning about our dharma), during my Darshan when he was camping in Tirupati, as he gave me two of Mahaperiyavas books without even me saying a word. I was overjoyed and overwhelmed by the sheer serendipity. As I have written about this in the book, I had to go back to him and get a verbal go-ahead for my peace of mind, as a subject as deep as our religion should not be treated frivolously. I thank all the great Rishis and Gurus who have contributed to our phenomenal religion called Hinduism for their wisdom, which I have used, to write this book.

I thank my parents and grandparents for instilling dharmic values in me by performing pujas, rituals and rites with devotion, which I have grown up observing whether at first I understood them or not. Today I see the value of it all! I thank my mother for pushing me to do my Sandhya Vandhanam every day and telling me how important it is. I thank my Dharma Patni Vidya for being the one to get me started on my writing journey in my darkest days during Covid, in 2021. She and her parents (My in-laws) have played a very important role in shaping my thoughts on our religion. I miss my father-in-law who is no more. I am sure he would have been thrilled to read this book and would have also given me guidance on various topics I have covered, from the Ramayana's perspective on which he was an authority, having studied and done the Ramayana Parayanam countless number of times in his life.

Last but not least, I would like to thank Shri Dushyanth Sridhar a very well-read Vedic Scholar who is doing yeoman service to keep the light of Sanatana Dharma shining bright, for agreeing to write the Foreword for my book. His words definitely add credibility to my efforts, as I have worked very hard to present what little I know in the simplest manner, to help as many people and families as possible get back to their roots and start learning about this beautiful, timeless, inclusive religion called Sanatana Dharma!

CHAPTER 1

AM I WORTHY OF WRITING THIS BOOK?

Honestly, I don't think I am worthy of writing this book. I am just an ordinary guy who has zero knowledge of Hindu Scriptures. I am no Guru, I was born into a relatively affluent Tamil Brahmin Iyer business family. I do my Sandhya Vandhanam (The obligatory duty of every Hindu Brahmin done for the well-being of oneself and all people and creatures of the world) only twice a day (Morning and Evening), while I am supposed to do it thrice a day (I have only recently started doing the noon Madhyanikam along with my morning Pratah Sandhya). However when I do it, I meditate and recite the Gayatri Japam to see if I can connect with the Paramatma within, for the well-being of me my family and all creatures of the world. I do not have any knowledge of the Vedas and unfortunately haven't learnt reciting the Vedas through adhyayana (learning from a Guru by listening and repeating), which I should have done, to do my bit in keeping the sound of the Vedas alive, as a brahmin by birth. I am actually more of a Vaisya as a third generation entrepreneur and far from a Brahmin who is supposed to only recite the Vedas for the well-being of all creatures of the world. With the blessings I have from my Gurus Jagadguru Shankaracharya Shri Chandrashekarendra Saraswati Swamigal (referred to fondly by Bhakthas as Mahperiyava or Paramacharya), Jagadguru Sri Jayendra Saraswathi Shankaracharya Swamigal (Referred to fondly as Pudu Periyava by Bhakthas), Jagadguru Sri Shankara Vijayendra Saraswathi Swamigal (Referred to fondly as Bala Periyava by Bhakthas) and the guru of all Gurus Jagadguru Sri Adi Shankara Bhagavatpada, I am able to support financially (give back what I am merely a caretaker of in this birth) towards protection of Dharma by donating to Veda Patashalas, old temple maintenance and other Dharmic causes. Having said all this I have read books like Hindu Dharma by Mahaperiyava, read and watched his discourses, read some books on HH Ramana Maharishis teachings, Swami Vivekananda's teachings, Autobiography of a Yogi by Paramahamsa Yogananda etc. and also have formed my own insights and opinions on this beautiful religion called Sanatana Dharma or Hinduism. So if I am not worthy of writing this book why am I writing it? Firstly I started writing this book to learn more myself and to document what I know and learn for my own children (I hope they read this book someday). I also have this innate urge to share what little I know and understand about Hinduism, with the world, from a layman's perspective, with the humble wish to communicate directly to those who wish to start their journey exploring this beautiful ocean that is Sanatana Dharma. Why I feel this book will help people is because I know so little and what I write might just resonate with people like me who lead busy, mundane lives like me in the material world, but have a yearning to know the purpose of this human birth and a little more about this religion. I want parents to read this book and share the knowledge with their children to make them proud of the beautiful religion they are blessed to be born into and guide them to achieve success in the material (Artha) and Dharmic areas of their lives. I will be donating 100% of the proceeds after income tax, that I receive as sale proceeds from this book for Dharma karyangals and Hindu causes. I am stating this to make it 100% clear that I have zero intention to monetize this work or make any money from the sale of this book.

I ask for your forgiveness and the forgiveness of the almighty Paramatma and Gurus if anything I have written in this book hurts anybody or is incorrect. That is not at all my intention. I am human, and I write based on my limited knowledge and interpretation of Sanatana Dharma which is too vast a subject for a mere mortal like me to understand even .00001% of in this lifetime.

CHAPTER 2

WHY THIS BOOK?

I have written two books on worldly subjects, and when I went to see my Guru (His Holiness Vijayendra Saraswati Swamigal aka Bala Periyava of Kanchi Kamakoti Peetam) when he was camping at Tirupati in March 2024, I had a thought in my mind to write this book about Sanatana Dharma. On that occasion I was lucky to get a personal darshan with my Guru and like he read my mind (which Gurus often can and do) he gave me two volumes of Mahaperiyava's Chennai Discourses. I was thrilled and took it as a sign to write this book . Though I immediately started writing this book, I wanted to get a verbal go ahead from my Guru as this is a subject that is based on religion and must not be treated lightly, and hence I went to Kanchipuram to see him again in May 2024. This time I asked him if I could write this book based on my limited knowledge and experiences, and he lovingly in his inimitable style smiled and asked me to go ahead and gave me two more books for reference.

We live in the Kali Yugam and I have been pained to see the forces of adharma rampant all around me. There is so much hatred for dharmic thoughts and a vicious campaign against Brahmins in specific and Sanatani Dharmic Hindus at large, as we are the easiest to spit venom on with almost negligible retaliation. I wanted to write this book to share my little knowledge on the unifying aspect of the Advaita Philosophy of Sanatana Dharma that I have been born in to by the grace of God and what I have learnt by reading books written by Gurus (or books of their discourses) like Bhagavtpada Jagadguru Adi Shankara, Paramacharya, Ramana Maharishi, Paramahamsa Yogananda, Swami Vivekananda etc. Having been a meditator and gone to the depths of anxiety due to health reasons post covid, I have seen and later missed the bliss of being able to meditate and feel bliss. The Adviata philosophy simply put says that the Jivatma (The consciousness that keeps our body alive) and the Paramatma (Universal Consciousness or God) are one and the same. So basically every living creature, every human being irrespective of their caste, creed, sex, religion, orientation have the same Paramatma within and we are all one. What thought or philosophy can be more inclusive and unifying than this thought that has been handed over to us by the great Adi Shankara? Mahaperiyava has said in his discourses that because of Bhagavatpada Adi Shankara, 57 Kingdoms and Bharat as a whole got unified because there were constant wars over ideologies and a battle for supremacy within the Hindu religion. The state of affairs apparently was so bad that the very survival of Hinduism had become doubtful. But the Advaita philosophy if understood and experienced shows us that you can worship an Ishta Deivam or not worship at all, but we all have the same Paramatma within us. So I wanted to write this book to unify all people of Bharath and the world at large by saying nobody's way is greater or lesser than the other, and the Sanskrit sloka of Ekam Sat Viprah Bahuda Vadanti which means that the paths are many but the truth is One is the only truth that we must accept for world peace.

CHAPTER 3

WHAT IS SANATANA DHARMA?

Sanatana Dharma or Hinduism is the world's oldest living religion. While many say it is a way of life, it is a way of life because it is a religion with no beginning or end. As Kanchi Mahaperiyava puts it, the beginning of Sanatana Dharma are the Vedas, but the Vedas themselves are Apurusasya and Anadi (Orphan), meaning they were not written by any one person and don't have an author. Most religions in the world have one person who founded it, Sanatana Dharma has thousands of schools of thought but a common culture that binds all its practitioners despite not having any single authority to command us. The sound of the Vedas always existed, are timeless and our great rishis and saints discovered them (mind you they didn't write them but discovered them) and shared them with the world for the well-being, peace and prosperity of all living creatures. Some people say the Vedas were discovered in 6000 BC, but the truth is nobody can trace the exact origins of the sound of the Vedas and our Vedic religion has been in existence since the creation of the cosmos and was arguably practiced world over. Today archaeologists are finding sculptures and Shiva Lingas from more than 28450 years ago and Hindu sculptures are being unearthed from practically every continent on Earth. Following is a screenshot of a tweet by KK Mohammed, a fantastic Indian Archeologist who speaks the truth and has helped us greatly in getting back our Ram Mandir in Ayodhya:

K. K. Mohammed @K_K_Muham... · 2d
The Kalpa Vigraha (Lord Shiva Hindu idol) is the oldest idol discovered so far on earth. University of California Radiation Laboratory, Berkeley which conducted the carbon dating of the wooden box that contained the idol and organic deposits in crevices of the idol itself 1/2

106   2,819   6,731

K. K. Mohammed @K_K_Muham... · 2d
indicated that it was at least 28,450 years old. This means that the idol was not even from the Kali Yuga. It was from a previous Yuga called the Dwapara Yug. None of the ancient civilizations of Egypt, Greece, Mesopotamia or Mohendojaro-Harappa had even begun at that time. 2/2

The Vedas namely Rig Veda, Yajur Veda, Sama Veda and Atharva Veda are cosmic sounds that have been captured through deep meditation and penance by rishis and passed on from Guru to Shishya orally, preserving the correct pronunciation, intonation and sounds (Svara). Our scriptures talk of the Yuga cycle consisting of 4 Yugas - Each Yuga Cycle lasts for 4,320,000 years (12,000 divine years. 1 Divine Year= 360 Years on Planet Earth) with its four yugas: Krita (Satya) Yuga for 1,728,000 (4,800 divine) years, Treta Yuga for 1,296,000 (3,600 divine) years, Dvapara Yuga for 864,000 (2,400 divine) years, and Kali Yuga for 432,000 (1,200 divine) years. So the start of each Yuga cycle is the exhalation or the breath of the Paramatma or big bang as science says today. Whether the big bang created the universe or signaled the end of the previous universe as some scientists like Nobel Laureate Roger Penrose say, Sanatana Dharma's wisdom shines bright as we believe that the cosmic cycle (split into 4 Yugas) is created, expands, contracts and then repeats all over again with the Paramatma's breath (exhalation- creation / expansion and inhalation-contraction and end), over 4,320,000 (4.32 Million) earth years. No matter what, we know that the cosmos is created and sustained by sound vibrations- everything is energy and we know even the smallest of atoms vibrate and today quantum physics studies energy at its most fundamental level. Human beings too are complex energy structures and our rishis went a step further and realized that every thought has a vibration and an energy impact, as our brain and nervous systems are made up of neurons and synapses that transmit electrical impulses. Sounds have an impact on our physiology, psychology and our energy chakras, as modern scientists now accept (music and sound impact on the brain and well-being are being researched widely across many top universities in the world), and our Guru Parampara have experientially understood this and have preserved this to date in Bharath, despite centuries of Mughal invasions and British rule. So Sanatana Dharma encompasses the righteous way of living for a peaceful and prosperous world. Sanatana Dharma spans daily life and rituals to situational leadership to lead a Dharmic life through Itihasas like Ramayana and Mahabharata to mutual acceptance of the whole world as one family (Vasudeiva Kutumbakam) for world peace. I personally do not know of any other living religion that accepts without questioning, all paths as true. Mahaperiyava in his discourses has said that different religions evolved in different times and in different parts of the world based on the basic nature and disposition of people in that time and those parts of the world. How Sanatana Dharma started and how it has sustained the onslaught of so many foreign religions without ever converting anyone from any other religion into its fold (unless people on their own start adopting the Sanatani Dharmic way of life by seeing its universal appeal), is a miracle and force of nature, as it resides in the hearts of the people of Bharath and all those who still call themselves Hindus world over. While the world merely tolerates other religions we Hindus accept all religions as true. Tolerance means 'I know I am superior but I will tolerate you and your faith'. Mutual acceptance on the other hand means that I wholeheartedly know that all faiths (religions) lead to the same ultimate truth and the One True God! So anyone lecturing us Hindus on mere religious tolerance or secularism is like a human being teaching a fish how to breathe under water!

CHAPTER 4

WHAT IS THE PURPOSE OF THIS HUMAN LIFE?

I have from a young age pondered on this question, till I read and heard a speech by Mahaperiayava. After reading and listening to his divine thoughts I understood that the purpose of this life is to experience Kama (desire) and Artha (Wealth and purpose), both pursued in a Dharmic way and then completely overcome them to attain Moksha (liberation). So in essence the purpose of this life is to become one with the Paramatma within us and prevent future births. The physical world is imperfect and our body and mind are perishable. The body can get diseases, can get hurt and can get killed, but the omnipresent, omniscient Paramatma (consciousness) in us has no death. The fundamental aspects of Sanatana Dharma is that we take on the physical body and are born to certain parents, a particular family, are born in a particular geography / country / religion based on our past life Karmas (Actions). The good that we experience in this life depends on the good deeds or Karma that we have accrued and the bad that we experience is a result of the bad deeds that we have committed in this life or the past. So if we have to completely avoid suffering we must achieve a state free of desires and one of detachment, that prevents us from the need to take on another body and go through the trials and tribulations of the physical world and escape the cycle of birth and death for good.

How do we know Karma is true?

The best example of the Karma theory being true in my opinion is again an explanation by the Mahaperiyava to a foreigner. A foreigner (a Christian by faith) who had come for the Darshan of Mahaperiyava at Kanchi, asked Periyava how he could prove that there is life after death because in Christianity this concept doesn't exist. Periyava after some contemplation told the foreigner to make a visit to all the hospitals in Kanchipuram the next day and make a list of all the babies that were born at a particular time that morning and come back to report to him about them and their families. The foreigner complied and got back to see periyava in the evening. Periyava asked him about what he had seen. The foreigner told periyava that one child was born to well-to-do parents, one child was born to very poor parents in a Government hospital, One child was born without a limb, so on an so forth. Periyava after patiently listening to the man said, all the babies born in the same geography at the same hour would have the same horoscope astrologically. He continued to ask, why then were the children born into such differing circumstances, families and health? Periyava went on to say that the Lord is ever merciful so why does he create suffering for some of the children and a very happy circumstance and family for some children? The foreigner had no answer. Periyava concluded that it is based on past life Karmas (good and bad) that the babies take on their physical form in this birth and hence the Karma theory of prior and future births of Sanatana Dharma holds true. The foreigner was spellbound!

CHAPTER 5

ARE WE POLYTHEISTS? WHY DO WE HAVE 33000 GODS AND GODDESSES?

The biggest weapon of the Abrahamic faiths to discount and discredit Hinduism or Sanatana Dharma is that we are polytheists and we worship stones, while they worship a single true God. The truth is even the Abrahamic faiths fight between themselves on whose God is the true God. The fact that they even fight between sects like Shias, Sunnis, Bohras, Ahmedias, Sufis and Roman Catholics, Syrian Christians or broadly the 6 sects of Christianity the Church of the East, Oriental Orthodoxy, Eastern Orthodoxy, Roman Catholicism, Protestantism, and Restorationism, on whose way to their true God is best. This is no different from some people of our Varnas (Castes) fighting over whose way is superior. The Mudaliars, Chettiars, brahmins-whether Iyers, Iyengars, sharmas. pundits, bhats etc, Kshatriyas, Vaishways, Yadavs, Schedule Castes, Schedule Tribes all have different practices but one thing that beautifully unifies us all is the umbrella called Sanatana Dharma and the unifying tenets of the Advaita Philosophy of the Vedas, that Adi Shankara painstakingly popularized during his short life of 32 years by walking the length and breadth of Bharath to unify us all. However the Abrahamic Faiths latch on to the fact that they have one God and we have many Gods and we follow a satanic religion. Nothing could be further from the truth, because as per Adi Shankaras teachings based on the timeless Vedas, no matter which deity one worships, they are worshipping the one and only Paramatma in a form whose characteristics they love and relate to. So what we must clearly explain to our kids and the next generation is that no matter who our Ishta Deivam or Ishta Devata is, we are merely worshipping one form of the Paramatma within us. So this philosophy transcends all differences of castes, creed, race, religion, sex, orientation etc. as all paths lead to the same Paramatma who may be referred to as Shiva, Vishnu, Brahma, Ganesha, Lakshmi, Saraswati, Allah, Jesus, Buddha, Guru Nanak etc. **So do you see how Sanatana Dharma is not polytheistic?** The best part of Hinduism is that we have no necessity to convert anyone or change anyone's practices as we believe all paths lead to the same truth or God within till a person practices his/her faith without the need to coercively or by force convert them to their faith.

Now, old temples built as per the agama shastras are also energy centres that help the spiritual seeker and even spiritual novice progress spiritually by impacting positively the energy centres (Chakras) in our body.

A deity helps the small child relate to God in a form that he or she loves and makes him a friend. A concept of a formless God is very hard for a child to relate to and love, hence as Swami Vivekananda says, Sanatana Dharma is a religion that caters to the spiritual novice as much as it caters to jnanis and realized souls who have experienced Jivan Mukti and found bliss by becoming one with the Paramatma while still in their physical body and mind.

So does this mean we are against Polytheism?

The short answer is 'Absolutely not!'. The beauty of Sanatana Dharma is that we are against nobody and against no school of thought. Why should we be against a child who hasn't learnt to walk? Polytheists are born in a particular religion based on their spiritual maturity. They too over multiple births will slowly realize Nirguna Bhakthi or the formless Paramatma. All soul journeys are spiritual, and Sanatana Dharma does not say my way or the highway like many organized religions. This is the absolute beauty of Hinduism and is a path to true world peace where we can peacefully coexist with every religion without the need to convert them to our path.

CHAPTER 6

UNITY IN DIVERSITY – NOT SAMENESS

Reformists want sameness but the differences exist for us to transcend them and realize that the external appearance and body are a result of past life impressions (vasanas), but the omnipresent, omniscient Paramatma (irrespective of how you call him or her) within each of us and all living creatures, is one and the same. So in the modern world the new buzzword is DEI (Diversity Equity and Inclusion), but Sanatana Dharma has been an advocate of DEI since time immemorial. Reformists tarnish Sanatana Dharma as casteist and there is no doubt that wherever there are people they will make even a perfect system corrupt for their one-upmanship. However through this book I would like to emphasize and reemphasize the thought of realized souls that there is ABSOLUTELY NO SUPERIOR OR INFERIOR CASTE OR RELIGION. There is no superior or inferior person irrespective of their gender, orientation, religion, caste, creed or race.

The physical body is a mere T-shirt that we wear during our soul's physical journey. We take on a body based on our past Karma and leave the body behind to take on another body (Maybe in a totally different country, following a different religion, in fact it need not even be a human body in the next birth!). This is the depth of DEI and oneness of Dharmic thoughts and Sanatana Dharma. What we must realize is that getting a human birth itself is a 1 in a Billion probability and we must not waste it without understanding the purpose of this birth (which only humans have the capability to), which is to realize God and avoid future births.

CHAPTER 7

IS SANATANA DHARMA A PERFECT RELIGION?

The physical world we live in is an imperfect one. There can be nothing perfect in an imperfect world. So even if for the sake of discussion we assume that Sanatana Dharma is a perfect religion, the people following it many-a-times are not. So I would take a nuanced view and say that like all religions of the world, we too have had our flaws and continue to have flaws as a people. What is however amazing about Sanatana Dharma is that there is no one way that is considered superior or inferior. While there have been Brahmins who have thought and continue to think they are superior, there are clashes between the Vaniars, Thevars and Dalits and the Jats of Haryana. There are Kshatriyas who believe they are superior and Chettiars who think so too (We have 3000 castes and 25000 sub castes and people of practically every religion living in India- All of them are proud of their varna, religion and way of life and that is fine till the thought of superiority or inferiority comes in). So, while there are issues of people who do not understand Sanatana Dharma fully, the dharma itself is all encompassing and I can say with conviction that nobody – not the smallest ant, the biggest elephant, followers of other religions, any caste are inferior or superior (I know this based on how the realized Gurus of this land have always treated people as one). We must all first and foremost eliminate from our minds any feeling of superiority or inferiority as we are all spiritual beings on one of many physical journeys. So if all of humanity understands this, which is at the core of Sanatana Dharma, yes, Sanatana Dharma is a perfect religion.

CHAPTER 8

SCIENCE BEHIND OUR RITUALS, YOGA AND MEDITATION AND WHY HINDUISM HAS ALWAYS BEEN SCIENTIFIC AND PRO SCIENCE

Some people might call things that I say pseudoscience. So be it, as I am merely sharing my experience and opinions and will leave it to the reader to accept or reject what I say. I have written this book from my plane of awareness and experiences and I need not be correct with all my observations as I am no realized soul or Guru. Having said this, as Mahaperiyava states beautifully, while an animal might not know the laws of physics, imagine if the animal says the laws themselves don't exist at all. Similarly we must accept with faith the lofty truths that our rishis have discovered and passed down to us whether we can intellectually understand them or not. Certain things can only be understood experientially and through practice without letting our ego come in the way.

Here I try to explain certain things that I intuitively feel are scientific based on recent studies and some from my research and readings of great souls who have walked the land of our great nation Bharath.

For starters let me bring to your attention a recent scientific finding that I will try to explain and extrapolate based on my limited understanding of Sanatana Dharma:

Interesting recent progress from the scientific world that I wish to connect with my highly limited knowledge-

Recently scientists are beginning to understand that consciousness is a continuum, and they are trying to measure it. The article in The Scientific American can be found in the following link:

https://www.scientificamerican.com/article/consciousness-is-a-continuum-and-scientists-are-starting-to-measure-it/

I will give you a gist of this scientific research and article for purposes of context:

Scientists have been trying to unravel what it is to be conscious and what exactly is consciousness? To study this, scientists in different universities have been studying what it means to be awake, asleep, under anaesthesia etc. Quoting from the article "In our study, we wanted a more sensitive and precise approach to measuring the onset of sedation without the risk of disrupting the transition. So we turned to a method first described in 2014 by sleep researchers at Massachusetts General Hospital and Johns Hopkins University. In that work, the investigators asked participants to squeeze a ball whenever they breathed in. The researchers tracked each person's squeezes using a dynamometer, a tool for measuring grip strength, and an electromyography sensor, which measures muscle response. In this way, they were able to precisely track the sleep onset process without disrupting it.

For our study, we trained 14 healthy volunteers in that same task and presented the breathe-squeeze exercise as a kind of mindfulness meditation. We instructed the participants to focus on their breathing and to squeeze a handheld dynamometer whenever they breathed in. After a few minutes of training for each person, we placed an intravenous catheter in their arm to deliver the sedative and set up vital sign monitors and a fitted 64-channel EEG cap to record brain waves throughout the experiment.

All participants reliably synchronized their squeezes with breathing during an initial baseline period without any sedation. They then received a slow infusion of dexmedetomidine, a sedative commonly used in operating rooms and intensive care units. As brain concentrations of dexmedetomidine increased, participants occasionally missed a squeeze or mistimed it. Eventually, they stopped squeezing altogether.

Following some additional tests, we turned off the dexmedetomidine infusion, allowing participants to recover from sedation. **To our astonishment, after a period of 20 to 30 minutes, everyone remembered the task and began spontaneously squeezing in synchrony with their breath without any prompting. This allowed us to analyse both the sedation-onset and sedation-offset timing and compare them with previous studies that used verbal commands to assess consciousness.**

The breathe-squeeze task was clearly a more sensitive approach to measuring the transition out of connected consciousness. Participants stopped performing the task at lower dexmedetomidine concentrations than those at which people had been observed to stop responding to auditory cues in other studies—highlighting the arousing effects of external cues on the system. These findings may also indicate that connected consciousness can be further broken down into internally generated behaviours (such as reminding yourself to squeeze a ball as you inhale) and externally prompted behaviours (such as responding to verbal commands) with separate transition points—an idea that refines our understanding of the continuum of consciousness."

So, Sanatana Dharma has always told us that consciousness is a continuum with no beginning or end. So, with my limited understanding I understand it as follows and am sharing it with you the reader for your understanding and further experiential enquiry through sadhana and meditation:

Aham Brahmasmi - I am consciousness

Brihadaranyaka Upanishad 1.4. 10 of the Shukla Yajurveda: [1.4. 1]

Tatvam Asi - I am that

Chhandogya Upanishad of Sama Veda

Science: Consciousness is a continuum.

My amateur Inference:

I am not the mind; I am not the body. However, Jivatma (the life force that keeps the body conscious) and Paramatma (God or Universal Consciousness) are one and the same - Advaita Philosophy.

Brief inference of recent scientific finding: Anaesthesia delinks the brain and the bodily response but does not eliminate consciousness or prakriti (universe) within us, and hence the body continues the ball clenching and breathing exercise once the body comes out of the effect of anaesthesia.

Adding to this: The impressions/tendencies/habits or vasanas that we accumulate during our time in the physical world tend to carry forward to future births when we take on new physical forms also, further connecting the Karma theory with continuum of consciousness that science is now talking about. The objective of this life is to realize the Paramatma within and realized souls transcend this time space barrier by connecting their individual consciousness to the universal consciousness (both being the same energy /God or consciousness. This unification is the ultimate goal of yoga, pranayama and meditation). While this sounds easy theoretically, God only knows how many lifetimes we mere mortals need to attain liberation or Moksha from this cycle of birth and death!

The beginning of the Universe – Sound and Creation

Preserving the sound of the Vedas is our topmost priority for the well-being of the world as per Sanatana Dharma. Science accepts that it was the BIG BANG that created the universe. In Sanatana Dharma we say Brahma or Parabrahma's breath and the associated sounds created the universe which is the multiplicity (sentient beings of different sizes, nature and disposition) of the one Paramatma, in addition to the non-living objects. Science also explains that every object has a certain vibration, and sound is vibration. So our rishis through great penance discovered the sounds of the cosmos, and what is interesting is that the macrocosm or the cosmos and the microcosm (what is within every living creature) are said to be one and the same. So if every object has vibrations, creating sounds of that frequency should be able to create that particular object – we have realized souls who could materialize objects from thin air.

So we must understand that science and religion are not opposed to each other but complement each other. So the sound of the Vedas, help in the inner vibrations of our energy centers and bring them in tune with nature. The combination of sounds and the control of one's breath through Pranayama helps us still the wandering mind and slowly realize bliss (Paramatma) within. So like electromagnetic waves are converted to sound waves today in mobile telephony, we must accept with faith that our Seers were able to grasp the sounds of the cosmos and share it with us for the well-being of the entire world, and hence they must be preserved and passed on from one generation to the next orally as every Sruti matters, and reading it from a book and learning could cause adverse effects to us and others if intonations (svaras) are changed. So the Vedic mantras are not only for this life but to help us slowly transcend this life and become one with the Ultimate Truth.

Moving on to yoga and meditation.....

Yogic science explains the importance of pranayama or breath control to calm/still the mind. All the asanas are to prevent the body from becoming an impediment to spiritual sadhana and unifying the individual consciousness (Jivatma) to universal consciousness (Paramatma). I have been a meditator for years but lost the ability to meditate post covid for almost 2 years due to crippling tinnitus, anxiety and a vayu imbalance as per Ayurveda, and am just getting it back slowly by God's grace and the power of Ayurveda. So I have seen both ends of the spectrum and am in a position to share the importance of pranayama and meditation for physical, psychological and spiritual growth. Though I had had my thread ceremony, being a brahmin, at age 13, and did my Sandhya Vandhanam (The obligatory daily prayers including for personal and global well-being, that combine, the Gayatri mantra, meditation and yoga) till I started college, nobody taught me how to do the Pranayama and meditate during the Gayatri Japam! So, when I restarted my Sandhya Vandhanam in my 30s I had lost precious years of yogic sadhana that is best started before calcification of the pineal gland in adolescent boys (The Pineal gland is the third eye that enhances intuition and outer-worldly powers). I would greatly encourage parents to start off their children on this spiritual journey through yoga / mantra meditation to handle not only the stresses of life with equanimity but also slowly move inwards to attain bliss and peace of mind. Starting by the age of 7 or 8 is crucial and if parents know that there is a deep science behind all of this, we can guide our children to do it for their benefit. Later on whether they continue it or not is their soul journey and that is ok.

Meditation- Today there are several EEG studies on the brain of meditators and the tremendous benefits of meditating. According to neuroscience research, mindfulness practices dampen activity in our amygdala and increase the connections between the amygdala and prefrontal cortex. Both of these parts of the brain help us to be less reactive to stressors and to recover better from stress when we experience it. More than being a way to handle stress better, Sanatana Dharma shows us that meditation helps us transcend the physical and experience bliss, even if it is for brief moments of time. Being mindful in our day to day activities improves focus, clarity of thought and helps us attain a state of heightened awareness and live more fully, in a world full of distractions. At this juncture I should mention what Mahaperiyava points out, which you can experiment with- When you experience joy or elation you will notice that the passage of breath will be predominantly through your right nostril. When you are enjoying sensual pleasure the passage of breath will be through your left nostril. When you start meditating the breath will pass slowly through both your nostrils when you become calm. When you are completely absorbed in meditation at the highest level breathing itself will cease, but there will still be life. This is when the great awareness called Jnana or knowledge and the oneness of the whole cosmos will be realized.

The importance of rituals.......

A recent Harvard research has shown the psycho-social and health benefits of rituals (https://hbr.org/2020/04/the-restorative-power-of-ritual). Sanatana Dharma is full of rituals. While the Vedas (Jnanakanda) ask us to ultimately transcend rituals (Karmakanda), Mahaperiyava clearly says that rituals are absolutely essential till one reaches spiritual maturity. I doubt very much most of us have that spiritual maturity to stop doing the rituals which are beneficial to us and our family. Sanatana Dharma considers Air, Water, Fire, Earth and Ether sacred. Rituals use water, the sound of mantras and offerings into the sacred fire in most Pujas and Homas. When people perform Pujas/Homas / Last rites / Ceremonies we must understand that we are trying to get the blessings of astral / celestial beings which we cannot see or feel in the physical world. When a person passes away, their physical body is burnt and it becomes ash, but the consciousness or what we loosely call soul continues to exist in the astral/subtle plane. My pseudoscience understanding of ceremonies involving fire is that the sacred fire converts gross physical offerings into subtle that could possibly enter the astral plane? I don't know if I am right but I think on these lines. Now why do we use water and chant mantras? Our bodies are made up of 72% water, and some researchers now find that water has memory (though not 100% conclusive). So when we chant Vedic mantras and sip the water could it possibly have a beneficial effect on our physical, psychological, emotional and spiritual well-being? I believe so and it is up to you the reader to take my opinion or leave it, as I merely make guesses from my experiences and reasoning of why we use water and fire in our rituals. We also use camphor to do the mangal arthi and tulsi leaves in water for the theertham – both of which are known to be anti-bacterial and anti-viral.

Even assuming there are zero scientific benefits, a ritual in itself brings the family together to do something to look forward to and then enjoy a good meal after it is done. Summing up, I wish to make a point that Sanatana Dharma is not anti-science, in fact it is pro science and pro technology as it recognizes the importance of Artha and purpose in the material world. My Guru Bala

Periyava often tells youth to pursue anything they do in the material world in a dharmic manner and always help the needy.

In this chapter though, it is not about rituals, I would like to share how advanced we were in terms of science itself. We were way ahead of the western world but have failed to give our ancestors credit for their discoveries and knowledge. As Mahaperiyava points out in his book Hindu Dharma, there are few scientific discoveries that are not found mentioned in Varamihira's Brhat-Samhita.

How do heavenly bodies remain in the skies? How is it that they do not fall? We all think Newton gave us the answer to these questions. Nothing could be further than this from the truth. The very first stanza in the Suryasiddanta, which is a very ancient treatise, states that it is the force of attraction that keeps the Earth from falling.

In Adi Shankara's commentary about the Upanishads there is a reference to the Earth's force of attraction. If we throw up an object it falls to the ground. This is not due to the nature of the object but due to the Earth's force of attraction. "Akarsana-Sakti" is force of attraction, the power of drawing or pulling something. He talks about the breath where "Prana" which goes up and is pulled down by "Apana". So the force that pulls something downwards is called Apana. So the importance of Pranayama is to direct energy (Prana or life force) upwards against the natural force of gravity that makes Prana move downwards is my simplistic inference. Adi Shankara quotes the Upanishads and says the Earth has Apana Shakti – does this not mean we knew about gravity well before the time of Shankara around 500 BC? It's shocking that our children don't study about Adi Shankara or Vedas or Upanishads properly in history or philosophy! Such is the state of our colonized education system that praises westerners where credit is actually due to our rishis and timeless Vedas. These things help us understand that we had discovered various scientific facts well before the westerners did. Today we are in a sad state debating whether Sanskrit should be mandatory in schools or not. If it becomes mandatory, our children might understand our scriptures and know the truth. How can we allow such a dangerous proposition in this world of false propaganda and narratives right? We have to keep them slaves with an inferiority complex so they believe everything Hindu is superstition and everything western (even their religion) is great!

Going further, our Jyotisha Shastra (Astrology) knew about the planets and mathematical systems prevalent in the world today. How does our Panchangam know when an eclipse is going to occur with such accuracy? Don't we have to think about these things? I feel ashamed that I cannot read Tamil well or Sanskrit and have to rely on my mother or wife to read the Panchangam. How shameful is this! This is the result of purely western education. My school (an 'International School') didn't even have yoga (To be fair, most Indian schools didn't during the 80s and 90s, sadly)! It is our duty to teach our children Sanskrit (if possible) and their mother tongue, and make them understand what an evolved culture we come from.

At the beginning of the Kalpa all grahas (planets) are in alignment. But over the ages they have changed their course. When another Kalpa commences they will again be in alignment. The "Samkalpa" we do before a puja or ritual contains the description of the cosmos, a reference to the time-cycle and so on. Mere superstition? I beg to differ.

We also knew centuries ago that the Earth revolves around the sun because texts of Varamihira, Aryabhatta and others speak of heliocentric systems long before western astronomers and scientists. Until the 16th century Europe believed the Earth remained still at the centre of the Universe and that the Sun revolved around it (Nicolaus Copernicus a Polish Astronomer only in 1543 finally stated that the sun and not the Earth is the centre of the Universe). What's worse was they believed this is how day and night were created and if anyone opposed it they were burned at the stake by religious leaders. "It is the earth that revolves around the sun, not the sun around the earth" stated Aryabhata way back in 500 CE by using the view "Laghava-gauravanyaya". i.e. the Guru means big or weighty and Laghu means light or sishya. So the Laghu revolves around the Guru. He used Sastric terminology to understand and depict an astronomical concept beautifully. In the olden days European religious leaders were opposed to science and even burned scientists calling them heretics. It is a shame that today we quote the descendants of the very same people who make the preposterous charge that Hindu religion stood in the way of scientific advancement and that it ignored matters of the world because of its concern for the other world. As a matter of fact our Sastras are a storehouse of science. Isn't it time to tap into this knowledge to see how we can further advance modern science today? It is not mere pride of the past we should live in, but we must acknowledge and help our future generations study it to possibly achieve even more scientific discoveries for future generations. All in all Sanatana Dharma is pro science and not at all anti science and it has never been anti science or anti-seeking knowledge.

Without discounting any of the inventions of modern science that we enjoy today, let me list out some subjects that were taught in our Gurukuls and recognize our great rishis whose knowledge has been destroyed due to invasions and lack of knowledge of our scriptures and Sanskrit. The list has been taken from Dr. Anadi Sahoo's compilation:

Our ancestors were far ahead in time, technology, mathematics, science and beyond. Our history books didn't give them their proper credit so I am putting it out in my book here. It is very important to know what was taught in Gurukul:

1. Agni Vidya (metallurgy)
2. Vayu Vidya (flight)
3. Water Vidya (Navigation)
4. Space Science (space science)
5. Prithvi Vidya (environment)
6. Surya Vidya (solar study)
7. Chandra and Lok Vidya (lunar study)
8. Megh Vidya (weather forecast)

9. Substance Electricity Vidya (battery)
10. Solar Energy Vidya (solar energy)
11. Day night Vidya (day night studies)
12. Srishti Vidya (space research)
13. Astronomy (astronomy)
14. Geography Vidya (Geography)
15. Kal Vidya (time)
16. Geology and mining
17. Ratna and Metal Vidya (gems and metals)
18. Attractions Vidya (gravity)
19. Prakash Vidya (solar energy)
20. Strings Vidya (communication)
21. Vimana Vidya (plane)
22. Jalayan Vidya (water vessels)
23. Agneya Astra Vidya (arms and ammunition)
24. Biology Vidyas (zoology, botany)
25. Yagya Vidya (Material Science)
26. Vedic Science
27. Commerce
28. कृषि (Agriculture)
29. Animal Husbandry
30. bird keeping
31. Animal Training
32. Yan Mechanics (mechanics)
33. रथकार (Vehicle Designing)
34. Gemology (Gems)
35. Jewellery Designing
36. Dressers (Textile Science and Design)
37. Pottery

38. Lohkar (Metallurgy)
39. Takshak (Guarding / Security)
40. Art (dyeing)
41. Ayurveda (Ayurveda)
42. Razzukar (Logistics)
43. वास्तुकार (Architecture)
44. पाकविद्या (Cooking)
45. Sarathya (Driving)
46. River and Water Science (Water Management)
47. Indications (Data Entry)
48. Cow shed management (Animal husbandry)
49. Garden tents (Horticulture)
50. Forest tent
51. नापित (Paramedical)

This type of Vidya was given in over 7 lakh Gurukuls across Bharath. It is impossible to include all topics covered as they were so vast and exhaustive. We should read and understand the wealth of knowledge that was imparted in our Gurukils.

Know your ancestors and their inventions:

Father of Astronomy: Aryabhatta; Work - Aryabhattiam.

Father of astrology: Varahmihir, works; five principles, great Hora Shastra.

Father of surgery: Charak and wellness, function: Code.

Father of Anatomy: Patanjali, Work: Yogasutra.

Father of Yoga: Patanjali, Work: Yogasutra.

Father of Economics: Chanakya, Work: Economics.

Father of Architecture: Vishwakarma.

Father of Aero Dynamics: Mayasur, Work: Vastu Mirror.

Father of medicine: Dhanwantari first rendered Ayurveda.

Father of grammar: Panini, work: Grammar Deepika.

Father of theatre: Bharatmuni, work: Theatre.

Father of Kavya (Literature): Krishna Dwaipayan (Vedavyas) works; Mahabharata, Ashtadasha Purana.

Father of playwright: Kalidas, works: Meghdhootam, Raghuvansham, Kumar Sambhav etc.

Father of Mathematics: Bhaskar II, Work: Leelawati.

Father of War and Weapons: Rishi Parshuram, Works: Kalaripayatu, Sulba Sutras.

Father of story writing: Vishnu Sharma, work: Panchatantra.

Father of politics: Chanakya, works: economics, ethics.

Father of sexual anatomy: Vatsyan, function: Kamasutra.

Father of Philosophy: Sri Krishna, Work: Sri Bhagavadgita.

Advait's father: Adi Shankara, works: language (language), Panchadashi, Vivekchudamani.

Father of Chemia: Nagarjuna, Work: Pragnaparmita Sutras.

Father of Electricity - Rishi Agastya - Electro Voltic Cell

Father of Aviation Science - Rishi Bhardwaj - Aviation Science

Father of Gravity - Brahma Gupt II - Gravity.

Father of Pie Value - Rishi Baudhyan - Baudhyan Formula - Price of Pie (Pythagoras Theory)

Father of surgery: Chark and wellness, function: Chark code and others.

Father of Anatomy: Patanjali, Work: Yogasutra.

Father of Economics: Chanakya, Work: Economics.

Father of nuclear principle: Rishi Kanad, work: Kanad formula.

Father of Architecture: Vishwakarma, Work: Surya Theory.

Father of Aerospace Technology: Bhardwaj Rishi, Work: Aviation Science.

Father of Poetry Tradition (Literature): Krishna Dwaipayan (Vedavyas); Work - Mahabharata, Ashtadasha Purana.

नाट्यलेखन के जनक: कालिदास, कार्य: मेघदूतम, रघुवंशम, कुमारसम्भवम आदि।

Father of martial arts (warfare and weaponry): Parashuram, work: Kalaripayatu and Sulba Sutra.

Father of Chemistry (Alchemy): Nagarjuna, Work: Pragyaparmita Sutra.

Father of Cosmic Science: Kapil Rishi, Work: Statistics.

Acharya Varahmihir: Father of astrology, predicted the discovery of water on Mars 1500 years ago.

Acharya Bhaskar: He first used the decimal system, using the size of 'O' (a circle) to reflect the value of zero.

We can go on and on and on, but this is a glimpse of our great forefathers!

CHAPTER 9

THE MONKEY MIND

I look at our mind like it is God's trick to see it jump from one thought to the other. Most of us have very limited control over our thoughts and the mind keeps on jumping from one thought to the next. In my 30s when I restarted my Sandhya Vandhanam and meditation after learning how to do the Nadi sothanam pranayama (which is a part of the Sandhya Vandhanam) properly from a Guru, I could slowly see the world around me much better. My confidence, clarity of thought, discernment of right from wrong, peace of mind and intuitive abilities started improving. I could fleetingly achieve the no thought zone while meditating and feel bliss. As an entrepreneur I wanted all my employees to leverage these benefits and started encouraging everyone in my organization to meditate. All this was great, but somewhere I think I lacked the humility and probably foolishly thought I had control over my mind. Covid came and God I think showed me and laughed when I was not only hit by the delta strain but I was overcome by extremely severe tinnitus, panic attacks and debilitating anxiety. I realized how foolish I was to think that I had even achieved .000000001% of what our realized rishis and masters have achieved in terms of controlling the mind. Why am I telling you this? I am telling you this to let you know that we have absolutely zero control of extraneous factors and must be ever grateful to the Almighty for this human life and the very fact that we are alive and breathing. The mind can be ones best friend or worst enemy and I have seen it all. God probably showed me both ends of the spectrum to share with all of you -the need for utmost Bhakthi and humility in anything we do. I have always been deeply religious and always knew that I couldn't move even a little finger without the blessings of the Almighty, but what I knew in theory I have now experienced in my life. Though I am not 100% health-wise, I am glad that I am slowly getting back the ability to sit still and meditate and feel his blessings.

CHAPTER 10

THE IMPORTANCE OF MATHA AND PITHA

In Hinduism Matha (Mother) and Pitha (Father) are placed even higher than the spiritual Guru and God (Paramatma), who follow Matha and Pitha. The beauty of our religion is to ensure children respect and love the mother who endures 9 months of great physical and emotional turmoil to give birth to us. She cares for us till she is alive and is the key person behind bringing up dharmic children. The father is next because, he is the role model for children to emulate, in the way he does whatever he does with a sense of service and dedication to us his children, wife, parents and family. A good father is also one who is dharmic in nature and is always ethical in whatever job or business he undertakes. So the beauty of Sanatana Dharma is to literally put our parents on a pedestal because they absolutely deserve it. They are our biggest assets and nobody in the world can love us more than our parents in this physical life. Also what is most important is that in Sanatana Dharma the parents are your first Gurus and guide you and teach you right from wrong. Moreover in an open source religion like ours, family traditions, rituals and practices are the bedrock for a solid Dharmic society. So everything starts with a stable family that has a good mother and a good father who guide their children to become strong, values-based, ethical adults who contribute to the well-being of Bharath and the world at large.

As parents, we must set an example of what is Dharmic and what is Adharma in this world where dangerous ideologies can take us and our children far far away from Dharma and become self-centred and not care about the future generations who will suffer greatly if we do not set the right platform for our children before the world starts putting all kinds of dangerous ideas in their heads. A western education without cultural and religious education will lead to a confused generation who loathe their own roots and will try to fit in elsewhere but will never truly fit in. Dharma is not meek as Swami Vivekananda says, it is strong and it takes guts to be all embracing yet be able to take an unpopular stand when the crowd is following Adharma to fit in. This is the reason Lord Krishna tells Arjuna that he cannot become weak thinking about his brothers and elders when he has a duty towards fighting them and protecting Dharma. So, as parents we must teach our children to discern right from wrong and use their own judgement and intuition rather than falling prey to the loudest or most popular opinion. Today wars are not only fought on the battlefield like in the Mahabharata, Wars are fought ideologically too. We as parents have to ensure Dharmic ideologies flourish and are passed on to the next generation who are proud of their dharmic roots and heritage, because they know that they come from probably the ONLY faith in the world that accepts ALL religions as true. This however should not become a slap me on one cheek and I will show you my other cheek kind of submissive ideology. Sanatana Dharma is situational and one must know when to push back. One must push back without hatred if one is confronted with a situation to convert to another religion by force or coercion. The Kshatriya blood must come out if a woman is being harassed to protect her dignity. There are various facets to Sanatana Dharma and hence it is an ocean of how to live life Dharmically. We must introduce our children to Itihasas like Ramayana and teach them how much suffering Lord Ram endured to uphold Dharma and that we must do at least .00001% of that to make the world more Dharmic and peaceful.

CHAPTER 11

GURU BHAKTI – GURU THE ANTENNA TO THE PARAMATMA

The year was 2013 and I had taken my wife and 3 year-old son to Kanchipuram for a Darshan of my Gurus (Shankaracharyas) Pudu Periyava and Bala periyava. While we were waiting outside, in eager anticipation, Bala periyava suddenly walked out. There were a few people ahead of us, but when he came out, he waved to them and asking them to move, looked directly into my eyes and asked me and my family to come forward. I don't know how to explain it, but that one glance from a realized Jagadguru gave me goosebumps and changed something within me. I don't know why he called us from the back but that was a defining moment in my spiritual journey – I am definitely not special- we are all equal for Jagadhgurus like Bala Periyava. We all immediately prostrated and did a sashtanga namaskaram. I had found my Guru! While I had gone to the Kanchi mutt a few times before and was fortunate to have had the darshan of Mahaperiyava himself as a kid, this incident made me want to see Bala Periyava again and again. Something in me had changed and I don't know what it is but I had a feeling of compassion cover my entire being. The love, bhakti and sheer joy I feel while in his presence is till date inexplicable.

My father-in-law who was a devout Ram-bhakth and someone who had done the Ramayana Parayanam several times in his life told me that the Guru is like an antenna who connects us to the Paramatma within us. So when a sishya is ready the Guru arrives. All I can say is, please keep following Dharma and a true Guru will find you and guide you. I repeat that I am an absolutely ordinary person, with zero knowledge of our scriptures or the Vedas and am merely someone who is deeply passionate about our great religion and culture. I am writing all this because I want to share from personal experience of a normal human being who will probably have several more births due to the paavam (bad karma) that I have and am accumulating in this world knowingly or unknowingly. While I know I do not do any adharma knowingly, we mere mortals have a long way to go before we can attain moksha and escape this brutal cycle of birth, suffering, death and rebirth. In the Kaliyugam, the Bhagavadham says that those who do not know the Vedas and the Shastras will wax eloquent about them – am I one of them? I do not know, but this is the reason I keep repeating that I am a nobody and please do not think I know anything. Everything that I say in this book could be wrong, but I have the compelling urge to share what little I know. Coincidentally when I went to have the Darshan of Bala Periyava in Tirupati in March 2024, I had in my mind this urge to write a book on Sanatana Dharma that is relatable to everyone. While I had this in my mind, I did not verbalize it. I merely handed over my previous book which was on mundane material matters and was speaking of other matters to him, periyava gestured to someone to bring something. The person got two books and Bala Periyava blessed and handed over 2 volumes of Discourses by Kanchi Mahaperiyava. I was overjoyed and took it as a signal to proceed writing this book. As I write this book I am also learning a lot of things from the books that contain precious wisdom of His Holiness Jagadguru Shankaracharya Chandrashekarendra Saraswati Swamigal and his discourses on Bhagavatpada Adi Shankara's teachings. As mentioned earlier, I went back to Kanchipuram again to get a verbal go-ahead from Bala Periyava to write this book, as I wanted to be 100% sure of my Guru's blessings and green-signal before handling a subject as important as Sanatana Dharma.

CHAPTER 12

DO SUBTLE AND ASTRAL PLANES EXIST?

What happens when we die is a question that all of us ask ourselves at some point. What happens when our soul leaves this physical body? I was fortunate to have a dear, loving maternal grandfather Mr. S.Gangadharan who was a medium. A medium is a person who can establish a connection with and communicate with the departed. How did my grandfather know he was a medium? Listen to this interesting true life story I have heard many times from him during my summer vacations and when I was doing my engineering and MBA staying with my grandparents, uncle and aunt in Chennai. When my grandfather was around 8 years old, his father a Chief Engineer of the electricity department who oversaw the construction of the Mettur Dam, had gone on a world tour by ship. When he was away, the only medium of communication was through Telegram. A few weeks after his departure, world war 2 broke out and there was no communication from my great grandfather for several days. My great grandmother and my grandfather's family panicked, when someone suggested out of the blue that they try to contact my great grandfather's father who was no more. A person with a planchet/Ouija board walked into my grandfather's house and said we would need a medium to try this super-normal experiment to find out if my great grandfather was ok. Unfortunately none of the adults seemed to get any response from my great grandfather's father. So, someone suggested they give a pen to my grandfather – the 8 year old boy who could barely write sentences and try. They tried and lo and behold, the pen in my grandfather's hand wrote an answer to the question "Is Mr. Sundaram safe?" in my great great grandfather's handwriting!! The response was "Yes he is safe and you will receive a telegram at 2 pm tomorrow". Sharp at 2 pm the next day the postman rung the bell and there it was, the telegram stating my great grandfather was safe somewhere in Europe. Is your mind blown? Doesn't this show us that these astral beings operate on a different time-space continuum? Every time I tell this story and the multiple stories and experiences that my grandfather has shared with me, my mind is blown. SO I can say with conviction that souls exist in the subtle and astral planes and they are there for short or extended periods of time before they take on their next physical journey to expend their accrued karma. So why is this important to this book? In Sanatana Dharma we place a lot of importance to ceremonies and rituals when a person passes away and the monthly Amavasya and annual ceremony. It is very important to do these karmas to the best of our ability for the well-being of the departed and our families. While these things appear to be pseudoscience, based on my interactions with my grandfather, I see a deep cosmic connection between us and the departed and our shastras and great rishis have told us to perform last rites etc. for a reason. If you are interested in the subject you should read Many Lives Many Masters by Dr. Brian Weiss who has done a lot of research on this subject.

CHAPTER 13

HOW DO REALIZED GURUS TRANSCEND THE TIME-SPACE BARRIER?

I have personally experienced my Gurus being able to operate at a different frequency and having an ability to almost read my mind, know what I was thinking or speaking before I had their darshan and know the future while being the protective shield for me and my family. True Gurus are Deergadharshis (Have the ability to see well beyond what we mere mortals are able to). I will narrate a story that demonstrates this ability of Kanchi Mahaperiyava profoundly well. My mother's cousin (My Uncle) Dr. Mani Veeraraghavan has been blessed to have some out of world experiences with Mahaperiyava which he has shared with us and his experiences with the great saint are now also documented in a series 'Experiences with Mahaperiyava' on YouTube (Just Google 'Experience With Mahaperiyava by Dr. Mani Veeraraghavan). My uncle Dr. Mani Veeraraghavan was born into a Tamil brahmin family in Coonoor but had limited to no religious exposure, barring going to the Guruvayoor temple with his parents once in a year. Dr. Mani Veeraraghavan is today a leading endoscopist and endoscopic surgeon in Chennai. His first connection with the Kanchi Mutt started when Dr. Badri asked him to accompany him to treat Pudu Periyava (HH Jagadguru Jayendra Saraswati Swamigal) who was ill. When he reached Kanchi Mutt he saw an elderly man sitting there and in his own words, didn't even know who he was. Little did he know that it was the great sakshaat Paramatma (God himself) in human form -Mahaperiyava. Mahaperiyava kept looking at him and going away and the rational Dr. that my uncle was he was getting edgy and irritated as he didn't even have practice sitting cross-legged. After a long time he was asked to go in and see Pudu periyava. After he was done with the examination my uncle was again asked to come back and sit in the hall. People told him that he could not leave till Mahaperiyava gave him permission to leave. After a while Mahaperiyava gave him the prasadam and asked him to leave. In his interview he says, despite all the arrogance and irritation, on his way back to Chennai he felt a sense of fulfillment and if he had to die that moment he would be happy to go! My uncle was so far removed from religion that he hadn't even had the customary thread ceremony as a brahmin boy, but he got the opportunity to literally keep seeing the mahaan and experience this on his first visit to the Kanchi Mutt to carry out his duties as a Dr. Realized Gurus see the soul and don't care about external religious symbols or how pious we are or act. Hang on as things get even better....

Subsequently my uncle was called upon often and started visiting the Kanchi Mutt primarily as a practicing Dr. along with Mr. Bhaskaran. My uncle clearly states in the interview on YouTube that it is not that Mahaperiyava needed them but he gave them (my uncle and his team of doctors) an opportunity to be with him. Once when periyava was in mounam (a period where he wouldn't speak), he indicated to his people like he was ringing a bell. Nobody could understand what he was trying to say. After one week of driving all of his aides crazy, when my Uncle Dr. Mani went to Kanchi. Mahaperiyava with a child-like smile looked at my uncle and then his aides and indicated the bell saying he had referred to Mani (Mani in Tamil means Bell).

One day, Dr. Mani's younger son suddenly started complaining of a bad back ache that happened occasionally at first and then became more persistent. At this point my uncle took him to a senior orthopedic and after examining him, the Ortho said he feels there is some swelling and was a little concerned and said I suspect something serious and would like you to do a CT Scan (Back in the 90s CT Scans weren't a very common phenomenon as they are today). Being a Dr. himself, my uncle and his wife were shattered knowing the possibilities of what it could be. My Uncle decided not to take the CT Scan the next morning and instead put his son in the car and drove him to Kanchipuram for Periyava's Darshan. When they reached Kanchi Mutt, the Pondicherry CM was sitting outside and they had been waiting for over an hour and hadn't been called for the darshan of Kanchi Mahaperiyava. My Uncle and his family were waiting when someone from inside came out and said Mahaperiyava wants you to come in. When they went in and told him that the boy was having this health issue, Mahaperiyava looked at him, took a pomegranate in his and gave it to him and briefly touched the boy. Normally Jagadguru's don't touch anyone unless some medical procedure has to be done on them and doctors have to touch them. But in this case this was a deviation from the rules for my uncle's little boy. The boy ate the pomegranate given to him by Mahaperiyava on the way back to Chennai from Kanchipuram. The next morning my Uncle's son started complaining of severe back pain and my uncle fixed the CT scan but it got postponed for some reason. From the day after, the pain disappeared miraculously and never came back and they never did the CT scan! Such is the power of Jagadgurus like Mahaperiyava. My uncle and his team of doctors say it's a miracle and there could be no scientific explanation for what happened – such is the power of our Jagadgurus who have attained immense powers that can change what is not prarabdha karma (Karma that even Gurus will never alter as a person must go through the suffering for past deeds that have matured in this birth) and heal even major physical ailments with no logical or scientific explanation.

My uncle and several devotees of Mahaperiyava have noticed that he can literally read your mind and take thoughts out of your head and respond even before a word is uttered. My uncle puts it very beautifully in his video and says that there are other forms of communication that they (Jagadhgurus) are adept at that we mere mortals do not have the grasp of and can't even begin fathoming. In 1992-93 my uncle had the great fortune of living with Periyava in his quarters as part of the regular team of doctors who would treat Periyava's physical body and was even fortunate to eat the food made for Periyava. He keeps repeating in the video that he was the most unsuitable person to be there, but such is divine play and soul connection that pull people towards God through a realized Guru. Despite being in bed most of the time, when Dr. Mani was pulled in to helping find and renovate a Kamakshi Amman temple in Coonoor, Mahaperiyava was able to guide him as to the exact location of the temple, how old it was, who were the people who were looking after it etc. My uncle raised and donated money for the temple and the community did the entire construction of the temple and HH Jayendra Saraswati Swamigal (Pudu Periyava) did the Khumbabishekam for the temple. Post this my uncle and his team of doctors took charge of free medical help for 25 villages near Sunguvarchatthiram. A lady had donated her property in Chrompet Chennai to the Kanchi Mutt and under Mahaperiayava's guidance my uncle started a school for nursing. Mahaperiyava asked them not to give degrees to the women but take widows, destitutes and downtrodden women to train. So he said while they will be given gainful employment they must work for the upliftment of our society and not get degrees and leave the country. Such was Mahaperiyava's awareness to help people at the same time help our country's poorest of poor through them. Later on however degrees were given as it was an inevitable progression to get qualified nurses.

My uncle goes on to say that much of the time he was with Periyava, he was in mouna vrdham (vow of not speaking for extended periods) . Up to a point doctors were not allowed to touch the saint as is the practice (a silk cloth barrier would be used), but beyond a point my uncle actually held periyava's hand to feel the pulse (as Periyava gave him the permission), and describes the skin as if was a new born's and not that of a man who was nearly 100 years old. When Mahaperiyava was really ill my Uncle says he used to pray to him. At one point when my uncle who was trained in resuscitation and emergency care prayed to periyava as he didn't know whether he should compromise and violate the body (which the procedure would entail) and trouble Mahaperiyava. He didn't know what he should do and literally prayed that he wouldn't have to put Mahaperiyava on tubes, ventilator etc. As he was thinking and praying Bala Periyava (HH Vijayendra Saraswati, my current Guru) walked in, called my uncle and told him in tamil that "A doctor's duty is to keep people comfortable when they are alive and not to fight and get back people from Yama – The God of death". My Uncle was flabbergasted that Mahaperiyava through Bala Periyava had given him his answer on what to do and what not to do, without any verbal question from my Uncle. Mind blown right?

The day periyava attained Siddhi, my uncle had left for Chennai in the morning as usual and was to go to Kanchipuram at 1 PM. He got delayed because his car was given for service and it got delayed. Dr. Bhaskaran, who was on duty, told my uncle that Periyava was perfectly well and that he could take the day off. My uncle decided it is better to go and reached Kanchi late. As he was entering the room to take charge Periyava passed as though saying you need not have the guilt of violating my body. Such is the greatness of mahaans who even time their time of leaving their physical body without causing any discomfort or moral dilemma to their doctors. What was even more fascinating was after Periyava passed away on 8th January 1994 my uncle witnessed people from all walks of life and all religions come and pay homage to the great soul. He lived and embodied the spirit of oneness of Sanatana Dharma that Muslims, Christians, Christian priests, people of all castes, religions and economic backgrounds, fruit sellers, flower sellers, celebrities and anyone and everyone felt they had lost a father figure and Guru. The crowd kept pouring in well past midnight! At this point when my uncle came out to drink something, he couldn't go back in because of the crowd. He then got to his car and left for Chennai and got back home and cried like he had lost his own father. Such was the impact of Periyava on a person who had very little knowledge about Sanatana Dharma, Hinduism and Mahaperiyava himself.

My uncle goes on to recall that on 6th of May 1993 on the day of Mahaperiyava's Jayanti (Birthday), my uncle was travelling to Coonoor from Chennai where his wife and children were on holiday, when he met with an accident. He had multiple fractures and says he was very lucky to be alive as the accident was serious. His mother who was in Chennai received a call from Kanchi Mutt saying Periyava wanted to know if Mani Veeraraghavan was doing fine. My uncle's mother who hadn't heard of the accident yet (as there was no mobile communication back in 1993), said he was doing fine. About an hour later again there was a call from the Mutt as Periyava had asked my Uncle's colleague Dr. Sridhar about my uncle. Even at that point my Uncle's mother didn't know about the accident and said my uncle was doing fine. It was only much later when my Uncle was taken to Coimbatore and treated could he call his mother and tell her he had met with a bad accident but was doing fine. This is when my uncle's mother realized why Periyava had been enquiring about her son! Mahaperiyava who was a deergadarshi (Someone transcending time and space) knew his disciple had had an accident and was enquiring about him like only God (Paramatma) could! While this is an experience of one person, millions of people have had such experiences with Mahaperiyava. This is the power of a true Guru in Sanatana Dharma and we are fortunate to be born in Bharath where there have been 1000s of such great God realized souls who have walked this land. No science or logic can explain their awareness, intuition and timeless wisdom.

You can watch Dr. Mani Veeraraghavan's Experiences with Mahaperiyava on YouTube by visiting the link below. The video is in Tamil, but in this chapter I have more or less covered the contents of the entire video in English for those who do not follow Tamil.

https://youtu.be/bzlpTlIzVQc?feature=shared

CHAPTER 14

IS INTER-CASTE / INTER-RELIGION MARRIAGE WRONG? THE PURPOSE OF MARRIAGE

When all living creatures have the same Paramatma (Divinity) within, why do we have so many castes and so many religions? I have always wondered about this. It is when I read Hindu Dharma by Mahaperiyava that I realized that all these differences exist in this world of Maya (illusion) for us to transcend and realize that we are all one. In the previous chapter I spoke about my uncle Dr. Mani Veeraraghavan's close bond and experience with Mahaperiyava. My Uncle was born into a Tamil Brahmin Iyer family, but he married a woman who belonged to a slightly different caste. Did Mahaperiyava not accept him or his family because he had an inter-caste marriage? It was quite the contrary right? The soul is the same – it has no sex, no form, no race, caste, religion etc. The physical body we take on and the religion, family, caste (Varna) we are born in to depends on the Karma of our past lives. Having said this there are no superior or inferior Varnas as our realized Gurus demonstrate, but being born into a particular family we have certain obligations towards the well-being of the world and have to perform them for not only our well-being but the well-being of every creature. So is Inter-Caste marriage wrong? I have made an inference that there is nothing right or wrong but a matter of friction in religious/ spiritual progress that our Gurus see. When Mr. Sadashivam a Tamil Brahmin married MS Subbulakshmi who was from the Devadasi community, Mahaperiyava wholeheartedly accepted and blessed MS Subbulakshmi and told her that her voice would be eternal, which it is today. Did he not encourage MS Amma to sing soul stirring devotional songs that we all enjoy till today? Did he not bless her to sing Maitreem Bhajata for world peace at the UN? So why do our Gurus ask us to marry within our Varna or Caste as far as possible? I draw a novice's inference that it is to not only reduce friction in the marriage and ease our spiritual progress but also to ensure that we can as a couple fulfill our Dharmic duties of having been born into a particular Varna. Whether we like it or not, though we are all one, we are born into families in a particular country, belonging to a particular religion / caste with distinct family backgrounds and religious practices and traditions based on our past Karmas. Our Gurus want us to be as close as possible to our Dharma so we can fulfill the rituals ordained to us so we can grow spiritually as a couple without too many differences in opinions due to completely disparate religious practices. So inter-religious marriages increases this friction especially when children are born because one parent's religious views would be dominant and this could confuse the child and hence make him or her have to start from scratch their spiritual journey when the longing to understand the purpose of life invariably hits them at some point in their lives. So what is the problem with this we might say. Nothing at all, but I humbly accept that I do not have all the answers other than saying that lesser the friction in a marriage from a religious standpoint, the easier it is for the couple, the family and the children to go in an ordained direction to uphold Dharma. Why go so far as religion, just difference in food habits could cause tremendous friction in a marriage. If one partner is non vegetarian and the other is vegetarian what would the child be? Will the vegetarian allow the non-vegetarian to cook non vegetarian food at home? Would the non-vegetarian force the vegetarian partner to cook or eat non-vegetarian food? Could this impede a person's spiritual progress because food is Rajasik, Tamasic or Satvik? I am not for a minute saying non-vegetarian food is bad and vegetarian is good – but just highlighting the friction these differences can cause in a marriage. We will address food in the coming chapters because food guidelines in Sanatana Dharma were based on the nature of work a person had to do (E.g. Kshatriyas who had to be strong and fight could eat Non Vegetarian food while Brahmins interested in purely spiritual matters had to avoid non-vegetarian food and opt for the path of least harm and Sattvik food- Again very scientific). As Mahaperiyava has spoken and written on multiple occasions, religions were born based on the nature of people, their level of awareness, maturity and disposition in a particular country / geography. Our religion has no concept of conversion and has no beginning or end, but that is not the case with Abrahamic faiths. They grow by converting people into their fold. So imagine an inter religious marriage where one person wants to convert the other to their faith? Our Gurus discourage conversion as the act of conversion itself demeans the One true God, as we then accept that there is some God better than our God. Read that again – when there is only one God, while we can call him or her by different names, where is the need to shun the religion of our birth to convert to another faith? One way of looking at it would be to eliminate all religions, castes and differences and make sure only inter caste and inter-religious marriages occur. This is what the atheists would want. While in theory this sounds great, our Gurus knew that though we are one it is very important to understand that none of us are so spiritually aware or elevated to understand this 100% oneness and hence friction will occur in this imperfect physical world. Also, the objective of Sanatana Dharma is not sameness but oneness in diversity while following the religion of our birth without conversion, while realizing that we are all one. So in a nutshell, with my limited knowledge, in Sanatana Dharma which is super scientific and all-embracing, there is no right or wrong in inter-caste or inter-religion marriages, but these will never be endorsed as the way to go by realized Gurus because of the problems and spiritual /religious friction and confusion this could cause in the day to day life of the couple and their families. In Sanatana Dharma, a man takes a wife not only for carnal pleasure (which too is an important Purushartha in Sanatana Dharma), but as a helper and team mate to perform Dharmic acts for the well-being of the world and bring to the world children of good character who would in turn uphold Dharma. In Hinduism the marriage rituals irrespective of caste (Varna) have so much meaning that if one were to delve deep into them we would understand that all the rituals revolve around the union of not only two people but their families and their role in upkeeping Dharma or righteousness in their married life and bringing children of character who would in turn be guided by the parents to uphold Dharma. In the modern world and in the Kaliyugam, many of us seem to have forgotten the Dharmic aspects of marriage and are only focusing on the material and carnal aspects of a marriage, while important, they limit our spiritual progress and ultimate goal of preventing future births (Attaining Liberation or Moksha). Make no mistake, Kama is a purushartha within the bounds of dharma to bring about children (souls) waiting to be born to fulfill their karma. However, our Sastras were so progressive that they even talk about when to have intercourse within the bounds of a dharmic marriage and Mahaperiyava has stated it beautifully in his book Hindu Dharama in Part 18 Titled "Marriage" in Chapter 1 and I quote:

"What is the Sastric method to control the carnal urge? From the day of the woman's period there should be no intercourse for four days. Then it is permitted for twelve days. Again there should be no intercourse until the woman has her next period. Even during the twelve days mentioned above the couple should not meet during the full moon, new moon, on days conjoined by certain asterisms etc. If such rules are followed the couple will remain healthy mentally as well as physically". In a later chapter the Jagadguru says these days this kind of continence is not practiced and hence physical weakness has become common and neurophysicians prosper at people's expense. Nothing in our Vedas and Sastras were without thought, The impact of celestial bodies like the moon and planets and their impact on our psychology and physiology are very deep and meaningful if we bother to understand or follow rules even if we do not understand it yet.

In today's world of material excess, competition and egos, arranged marriages within the same community, love marriages within the same community and inter-caste marriages are all susceptible to issues. So, we must strive not to fight and be partners in Dharmic and material progress (Never forget man needs material objects and money for survival and Artha is accepted as a Purushartha as is Kama or desire that one must experience. However both Kama and Artha have to be practiced within the realms of Dharma). In today's world too much importance is being given to the monetary contribution of both partners that we are forgetting the finer aspects of family life. It is fantastic that today technology has made earning a livelihood a level playing field for men and women, but whether for a man or a woman, we must never forget that we work to live and don't live to work. We must do our best to get involved and help monetarily or with our time for Dharmic causes and involve our children in the process. Will our children follow our footsteps? As Lord Krishna says, Nishkama Karma is the way. We can merely follow due process and have no control over the result. Our children sometimes may go far away from a Dharmic life because that is probably their soul journey and they have to learn their lessons the hard way before they come back home to timeless truths embedded in our religion. So we must keep doing our work and set examples rather than lecture, and leave the rest to the Almighty. As I said earlier the purpose of writing this book is for my own children as much as it is for all people and all children who wish to lead a Dharmic life to the best possible extent in this modern frenetic world.

Another aspect that those who bash Hinduism will state is the fact that child marriage existed and it was a very bad practice. As Mahaperiyava says, marriages were conducted for spiritual progress of individuals and not for material and carnal aspects alone, and as a young boy would accept his Guru as his God at 7 years of age and surrender to him foregoing his ego, a girl would accept a qualified boy who had good character and well-versed in the Vedas as her God / Isvara before Kama hits her, foregoing her ego (An ideal albeit impossible couple to emulate are Lord Ram and Sita Maa, the epitome of Dharma). Mind you if you look at this from a western gender lens you might think it is against women, but if we understand that the soul / Paramatma has no gender then only we can understand this Atmic concept. Though the marriage would be conducted, the boy and girl would not live together till the girl attains puberty. But the boy and girl will be friends and grow up together but living separately with their respective parents (The age difference between the boy and girl would be 5-10 years). Santana Dharma gave a lot of importance to puberty and the importance of channelizing Kama or desire when it strikes the boy and girl in the proper way within the bounds of marriage without any shame of engaging in a happy conjugal relationship. Sanatana Dharma understood the importance of Brahmacharya (celibate student life to ensure focus and mental clarity without distractions), Grihastashrama (Married life where Kama and Artha are experienced within the bounds of Dharma), Vanaprastha (Retired life in a forest, soul searching), Sanyasa (Renouncing the material world and detachment). Today in a world of Tinder, delayed marriages and pre-marital sex where matters of the body seem to far outweigh matters of the soul, this topic is best not discussed in-depth as it can very easily be misconstrued and misunderstood. But in the so-called modern westernized world, are we not seeing the increase in teenage pregnancies, that harms the girl the most? **So let me keep it simple and say, today child marriage is illegal as it should be, because most people are not following a dharmic life or becoming so well-versed in the Vedas or their respective Dharma. Moreover most men are not in the dharmic path that a woman can take him as her Guru and surrender to him for spiritual liberation, like a man surrenders to his Guru by the age of 7 or 8 for his spiritual liberation.** If you are interested in this subject to understand why child marriage was used as a means of spiritual liberation especially of the woman, please read Hindu Dharma by Mahaperiyava (No this was not patriarchy as it was about the soul (Aatma) and not egoistic material pursuits and pursuits of desires alone like in today's world. Also other than the strict rules of marriage laid out for Brahmins, for other Varnas like Kshatriyas, Vaishyas, Shudras the girl could choose her husband in a Swayamvara E.g. How Sita Maa chooses Lord Ram and not the other way around. Even for Brahmins the boy's parents had to go asking for a girl in marriage after the boy completes his education in the Vedas and not the other way around). There were 8 types of marriage and you could read about them by reading Hindu Dharma by Mahaperiyava if you are interested). As parents we should try our best as Mahaperiyava says, to get our sons and daughters married at the earliest once they finish their college education (and hopefully some Vedic learning for boys and cultural, vocational learning for girls including Itihasas and Slokas), get some time to work in jobs they wish to **and they attain the legal age of marriage.** We all know this is easier said than done as we are all stuck in the materialistic race of life and we can only try to show our kids the way without trampling on their material dreams and hope their Karmas and soul journeys make them take the right decisions at the right time without harming their bodies, mind and inner self. Make no mistake, the reason for early marriage was to eliminate friction due to set ways and ego clashes that have become way too common sadly due to delayed marriages (We are more flexible and adapting when we are younger). Our rishis and Gurus knew the importance of channelizing sexual desire and satisfying it within the bounds of marriage as soon as it hits the boy and the girl, as suppressing sexual urge without proper yogic techniques could be dangerous. The idea was to channelize it, experience it, enjoy it with a loving partner and slowly yet surely overcome it for the next stage of life. The purpose of marriage was also to bring to the world souls waiting to be reborn and give them a chance to live out their accrued Karmas in a Dharmic manner.

Having said all this, drawing from the examples of our Goddesses like Saraswati, Lakshmi and Durga who hold the most important portfolios of Education, Wealth and Defense and people like Rani Lakshmibai and other great women of ancient India, we must make sure our girls are financially literate, enterprising, entrepreneurial (to create jobs for our country) and can stand on their own feet and shine in any sphere of life just like the boys do! However, neither man nor woman should become egoistic about their role, achievements, financial disposition etc. as this takes us very far away from our Dharmic path.

Thankfully both boys and girls are brought up the same way today (rightfully so) and girls and boys should be allowed to pursue their careers or be homemakers as they wish to, but while working as a team to practice festivals, doing daily/regular Pujas and doing their dharmic duties for the well-being of the world at large. We must understand that Sanatana Dharma was always progressive and we too must allow our children to pursue their dreams before and after marriage without putting caring for their families and children on the back-burner.

In Sanatana Dharma, family and dharma (spirituality) takes precedence over materialism and carnal pleasure, though materialism (Artha) and Desire (Kama) both are purusharthas and have an important role in the life of married couples.

So reformists may say do away with caste completely if we are all one. Atheists say do away with religion completely, if we are all one. While these thoughts sound great theoretically, it is impossible to stop people's longing for a higher purpose and God realization. Since linguistic divide in India is so bad, should we do away with all our languages? Is it not impossible? Hence Unity in diversity is the only solution for which Sanatana Dharma is a shining light if understood at its core.

The Importance and Science Behind the Gotra (or Gothram) System

Since we are on the topic of marriage, I feel it is important to cover an amazing scientific aspect of our Gotra System. Though we have discussed inter-caste and inter religious marriage, we have not discussed the importance of not marrying a person belonging to the same gotra. If we have an unbroken, traceable male lineage that is taught to our children, we will know our Gotra (or clan). A Gotra traces your lineage to a Sapta Rishi and their sub-lineages from the paternal side. Our rishis understood genetics and this is how they were way more advanced than we are, back in the day:

Those who are really interested in knowing about GOTHRAM

"GOTRA/Gothram" in HINDUISM Vs "GENE MAPPING!"

Do you know why every time you sit for a Puja, the temple poojari asks you for your GOTRA ?

The Science behind GOTRA (Genetics), is nothing but what is today popularly known as GENE ~ MAPPING.

What is the GOTRA system ?

Why do we have this system of Gotras ?

Why do we consider the knowledge of one's Gotra to be so important to decide marriages ?

Why should only Sons carry the Gotra of father, why not Daughters ?

How/Why does Gotra of a Daughter change after she gets married? What is the logic ?

In fact, this is an amazing and ancient genetic science that we follow. Let's see the SCIENCE of GENETICS behind our great GOTRA systems.

The word GOTRA is formed from two Sanskrit words, GAU (meaning, Cow) and TRAHI (meaning, Shed).

GOTRA means Cow-shed.

GOTRA is like a cowshed protecting a particular male lineage. We identify our male lineage / Gotra by considering to be descendants of the 8 great Rishi (Sapta Rishi + Bharadwaj Rishi). All the other Gotra evolved from these only.

Biologically, the human body has 23 pairs of chromosomes (one from the father and one from the mother). Of these 23 pairs, there is one pair called Sex Chromosomes, which decides the Gender of a person.

During conception, if the resultant cell is XX chromosome, then the child will be a Girl. If it is XY, then it will be a Boy.

In XY - X is from Mother and Y is from Father.

In this, Y is unique and it doesn't mix. So in XY, Y will suppress the X and the son will get Y chromosomes. Y is the only chromosome that gets passed down only between male lineage. (Father to Son and to Grandson).

Women never get the Y chromosome. Hence, the Y chromosome plays a crucial role in genetics, in identifying the genealogy. Since women never get the Y chromosome, the Gotra of the woman is said to be of her husband, and therefore changes after she is married.

There are 8 different Y chromosomes from 8 Rishis. If we are from the Same Gotra, then it means we are from the same root ancestor.

Marriages between the same Gotra will increase the risk of causing genetic disorders as same Gotra Y chromosomes cannot have crossover, and it will activate the defective cells.

If this continues, it will reduce the size and strength of the Y chromosome which is crucial for the creation of males.

If no Y chromosome is present in this world, then it will cause males to become extinct.

The GOTRA system is thus an ancient method devised by our great Maharishis to avoid genetic disorders and attempt to protect the Y chromosome.

Amazing bio-science by our Maharishis. Our Heritage is unarguably THE GREATEST.

*Our Rishis had the "GENE MAPPING" sorted out thousands of years ago.

So now do you see why the male child was special and protected? It was because of the weak Y chromosome. This then became an obsession and people wrongly started killing the girl child as they were considered a burden materially. So we have to educate people that neither boy nor girl are superior or inferior in Sanatana Dharma, but if same Gotra marriages take place there is a possibility of genetic defects and the weakening of the Y chromosome!

CHAPTER 15

IS RELIGIOUS CONVERSION ACCEPTABLE? DO WE HAVE CONVERSION IN HINDUISM?

Based on what I have learnt by reading the works of some realized souls like Mahaperiyava, Ramana Maharishi, Swami Vivekananda etc., I can tell you with conviction that Hinduism (Sanatana Dharma) has no form of conversion. A person following any faith may take to Dharmic practices based on their soul journey but with no formal procedure for any sort of religious conversion. So is religious conversion acceptable? Mahaperiyava explains religious conversion beautifully. He says, when there is just one God, if a person says my God is better than yours what does it mean? If a person listens to that and converts to another religion, does that not mean you feel there are more Gods than one and that you are changing your faith to the better God? Does it not demean the Almighty himself? Read it again and again to understand, as it has a very deep meaning. When people of different religions fight over whose way is superior,

Sanatana Dharma just says follow the religion of your birth and mutually respect all other religions and you will reach the ONE omnipresent, Omniscient Paramatma. So religious conversion is something that realized souls **do not endorse** and such a concept does not exist in Sanatana Dharma. There is but One God and we call him by different names is what Sanatana Dharma says, so why convert from one path to another? I recollect a story I read about a devout Muslim man who went to Paramacharya for darshan and Mahaperiayava asked him how many times in a day he does his Namaz. I have copied the text from the site I read it in, below:

Experiences with Maha Periyava

Namaskaram. I am Dr.Venkataraghavan, an eye surgeon. My wife, Gayathri Venkataraghavan is a musician and both of us owe everything in life to the boundless Grace of Sri Maha Periyava.

I just have an experience to share with all of you…

Many years back, a Muslim gentleman walked into my clinic. Seeing Sri Maha Periyava's photo, he bowed in reverence and mentioned that Sri Maha Periyava is a great sage. I was surprised and asked him how he knew about Sri Maha Periyava. The Muslim gentleman shared his experience which I shall present in the first-person account as narrated to me.

"Sir, I was a linesman in electricity board about 40 years back… We, in a group of 5 or 6, went to the Kanchi Matham to attend to a fault. Sri Maha Periyava who was seated there, gestured me to come and queried whether I prayed 5 times a day. I was shocked as to how Sri Maha Periyava could make out my religion. Sir that was only the beginning of my surprise. Then Sri Maha Periyava quoted from the Holy Quran extensively. We are Tamils who read the Quran. So, the Arabic that we read will have a Tamizh tint.

However, Sri Maha Periyava recited the Quran just as an Arab would speak his native tongue. His purity of diction was truly amazing, Sir If I had thought that this was great, then more was to come, he said.

Sri Maha Periyava then quoted a particular point and asked me how many times had the Quran mandated daily prayer?

I replied 5 times as any devout Muslim would. Sri Maha Periyava then asked me to get it clarified by the local Kazi. I did so and reported back to Maha Periyava, the same news. Maha Periyava then told me to get in touch with the Chief Kazi at Madras and get back to Him. The Chief Kazi not only said the same thing but chided me of asking useless questions. I reported the same to Sri Maha Periyava.

It was then that a great feat happened. Sri Maha Periyava asked for the Quran book to be brought and effortlessly showed and quoted from the Arabic that, actually mandated daily prayer was 6 times. However, since the 6th time falls at 11.30 pm many people skip it. He told me that if I prayed for the 6th time also, I would really benefit. Sir, true to His word, I retired as an executive engineer of EB.

Then when I had gone to Kamakshi temple for official work few times, Sri Maha Periyava would recognize me, bless me and Enquire Number of Times I Pray!!!

Just look at the Encyclopaedic Knowledge of Sri Maha Periyava the Omnipotent, Omnipresent God Who Walked. I was really blessed to have listened first hand to such a great experience.

Sri Maha Periyava has blessed countless souls irrespective of their religion.

I read up and found that the 6th prayer time is optional but beneficial for devout muslims and is called Tahujud and is at night (11:30 pm or after midnight is what I have read from various sources and I may be wrong). The point is realized souls of Sanatana Dharma guide people to follow their religion to realize God within. Whether we call him Paramatma or Allah or Jesus or Buddha or Shiva or Krishna makes no difference. This is the beauty of oneness that Sanatana Dharma is all about, so where is the need to convert anyone? I wish people of the world practice their faith without trying to forcefully or coercively convert anyone to their faith. This would definitely lead to world peace, but will this collective realization come? In hope we live....

CHAPTER 16

DIFFERENCE BETWEEN SAGUNA BHAKTI AND NIRGUNA BHAKTI

Sanatana Dharma is so beautiful that it helps the spiritual novice relate to Brahman (Paramatma) in forms that can be given characteristics. This makes relating to God and one pointed focus on a deity easy even for children and the spiritual novice that most of us are. This is Saguna Bhakti where we say I like the characteristics of Lord Ram, Lord Hanuman, Goddess Durga, Goddess Lakshmi, Lord Shiva, Lord Vishnu etc. So we have Puja rooms in our homes with many pictures and deities of these Ishta Deivams. Similarly old temples were built in high energy geographic locations as per stringent agama shastras to help spiritual progress of disciples who enter the sanctum sanctorum. These are not mere stones as people from other religions would say, but consecrated structures that have the ability to impact our psychology and physiology in positive ways. So worshiping the omnipresent, omniscient Paramatma by giving him a form is called Saguna Bhakti.

Now when people throw allegations at us saying we worship stones, we should tell them that the Advaita philosophy is all about Nirguna Bhakti where one meditates with his or her eyes closed and worships the Paramatma within us with no form or gender. This is Nirguna Bhakti. So do you see how our religion embraces the spiritual novice and takes him or her slowly but surely through one-pointed focus on a deity / deities first, and then inwards to realize that divinity or Paramatma is within us? Beautiful isn't it?

CHAPTER 17

IS SANATANA DHARMA PATRIARCHAL? WHY CAN'T WOMEN ENTER SOME TEMPLES? ARE WE AGAINST WOMEN EMPOWERMENT?

A common allegation against our religion is that we are patriarchal. Let me for a second accept it, but tell me which major religion in the world is not patriarchal? Having said that, which other religion worships the feminine like we do in Sanatana Dharma? Did you know that many Pujas, Homas and Ceremonies cannot be done by the man alone? He needs to have his wife by his side. While we are not perfect as people, we must not throw stones at such a beautiful religion that places the woman and feminine in an exalted position. The Sabarimala issue became a big problem and it became a political battlefield by telling our women that they were being discriminated against. Nothing could be further from the truth.

Our ancient temples are not mere stones as people from other religions would say, but consecrated structures that have the ability to impact our psychology and physiology in positive ways. This is the reason that some temples like Sabarimala are only for men and women of pre and post menstruation age and some Bhagavati temples are only for women. These are not discriminatory but actually protective measures for women and men respectively based on our physiology. Sinu Joseph author of Women and Sabarimala, a Christian woman has done tremendous work and research on why women should not go to Sabarimala and how it affects them adversely. She went and meditated at five of the Shat Chakra temples associated with Sabari Mala other than Sabari Mala to experience the impact and understand how the Chaitanyam of the temple impacts the female body. She says that every temple has a direct impact on the human body. Since it went to the Supreme Court, Sinu Joseph wrote a book to explain this and has also conducted a session for Supreme court lawyers handling the Sabarimala case. In a short video based on her research she says if women in the menstrual age enter the Sabarimala temple, they will definitely have issues with their reproductive health. She goes on to say that their periods cycle will get altered, they will have difficulty in menstruating and they could have severe menstrual disorders like PCOD or endometriosis. She explains the how and why of this in her book and we should all read it. There is one more Shat Chakra temple called the Aryan Kavu temple where women are not allowed beyond a certain point. When Sinu Joseph went there and had the Darshan of the deity she started tearing up despite the fact that she had never even been to many temples. She says this was very strange for her to experience. After this experience she goes on to say that her own cycle changed and that is the reason for these restrictions. She started her study from the Bhagavati temple in Chenganur and miraculously her period cycle aligned with the earth's fertility cycle, which means you get your period on Amavasya (no moon or new moon day). She says every woman in the menstrual age who visits the Bhagavati temple will see her health improve. Surprisingly when she went to the same temple the second time when there were 100 Ayyapa Swamis (Or men who take on the vow of celibacy and Vrath of 41 days before they visit Sabarimala) she found that her cycle was again disturbed. People may discount what she says as rubbish, but she emphatically says that if just the presence of Ayyappa Swamis can do that to a woman's cycle in a Bhagavati temple, imagine what could happen if one visits the powerful energy centre at Sabarimala! Whether one believes this or not, our forefathers were extremely scientific and delved deep into various aspects of human psychology, physiology and the impact of planets and celestial bodies on our well-being and how we could be in tune with nature for our well-being. Our ancient temples were constructed with these aspects in mind and I doubt very much we want to mess with such energy structures, for our own well-being. So Sinu Joseph goes on to say that the restriction of women in such temples like Sabarimala is for protection of women and for their fundamental right to health. So in a nutshell she says Sabarimala has been protecting women and not discriminating against women. Hats off to this amazing woman for going in depth and studying this and sharing it with the world. She says and I agree that we have to take immense pride in the fact that our religion is so scientific that every ancient temple has the capacity to impact our health through the chakras. The nature of the chaitanyam in temples affects women differently and men differently. While doing this study she researched other places where women were not allowed and found that Mt Athos in Greece and Mt. Omine in Japan which were both at an altitude of 5000 ft restricted entry of women of any age. She then delved into several American and European studies that show that altitude have an impact on women's reproductive health and fertility. On the way to Sabarimala, there is a place called Kari Mala at 5000 feet and hence she concludes why the 41 day yatra cannot be undertaken by women of menstrual age. So every tradition in our religion if we experience and contemplate will be for our own well-being. While we may never get all the answers, we must educate ourselves and our children that everything cannot be looked at from a western lens. Our civilization and culture is one of the oldest and most scientific and we must strive to understand why we do what we do and do our rituals with Bhakti and in an ego-less state even if we do not have a logical explanation, knowing fully well that our Gurus and Rishis were scientists who had understood the cosmos way better than we have in today's so called modern world.

To wrap up this chapter if we were against women and are discriminatory why are there temples like

The Chakkulathukavu Temple where there is a Naari Puja during which men are not allowed to enter? Further the list of temples where men aren't allowed to enter are:

Kumari Amman Temple in Kanyakumari

The Kumari Amman temple nestled in Kanyakumari has Maa Bhagawati Durga in its sanctum sanctorum. The temple permits celibate men or sanyasis to only enter till the gate of the temple. Married men are however prohibited from even entering the premises. This temple is believed to be the place where Mata Parvati did penance to gain Lord Shiva as her husband. Only women visit this temple of Kanyakumari Kanya (virgin).

Mata Temple In Bihar

Mata Temple in Muzaffarpur, Bihar only permits women during the time of "periods". The temple follows its rules so strictly that even male priests don't enter the temple premises during that time. The temple turns into a women-only zone as the goddess is believed to be menstruating then

Attukal Bhagavathy Temple in Kerala

Kerala's Attukal Bhagavathy Temple is one such temple in the country which prides itself to be a women dominant temple. The temple's Pongala festival, participated by millions of women even made it to the Guinness Book of World Records. This festival is regarded as the largest gathering of women for any religious activity. Pongala is a 10-day festival which falls between February and March. Here, women offer bangles to the goddess or devi.

So anytime there is a narrative that influences our children that Hinduism is anti-women, please explain to them that there could be nothing further from the truth than that. There are good people and bad people in all religions and families, that do not treat their women properly, but let us not hurl abuses at our beautiful religion that worships the feminine energy, as much as it reveres the masculine energy. Both have a symbiotic relationship in our religion.

Brahmaji Temple In Rajasthan

Rajasthan's Brahmaji temple is one of the most significant temples of Lord Brahma. Here, married men aren't allowed to enter this 14th-century temple. According to the religious texts, Lord Brahma performed a yagna at the Pushkar Lake. He had to perform this with this wife Goddess Saraswati. But since Goddess Saraswati was late for the event, he married Goddess Gayatri and completed the ritual. The infuriated Goddess Saraswati cursed the temple. She cursed that no married man is allowed to enter the inner sanctum, otherwise, trouble shall arise in his marital life.

Kamakhya Temple In Andhra Pradesh

Just like the famous Kamakhya temple of Guwahati, the Kamakhya Peetham in Visakhapatnam also denies the entry of men for some days every month. The temple bars men from entering for four to five days to observe the privacy of women during their period of menstruation.

Please share this with your daughters and sons so they know why we do what we do instead of belittling themselves and their own faith because wokeism is the new peer pressure and we as parents aren't teaching them how amazing our religion really is, for the simple reason we ourselves don't know! Now that you know, please share this knowledge widely and start really empowering our women not only for the material world but make them embrace their power of Shakti for spiritual progress too! Our women should never feel Sanatana Dharma is against them, because the TRUTH IS IT IS NOT! This is the easiest way for western powers to break our families and thereby the rock-solid institution that builds our great nation.

Having said this, the immediate retort from some highly liberal cousin, friend or family member would be, "What about Sati?". Great questions. We can't win all arguments but ask a reflective question about "Do you know what is Jauhar?". Most of our history books make the Mughals look like highly progressive feminists while we Hindus were women hating misogynists. Nothing could be further than that from the truth. The Mughals would take Hindu widows as concubines, rape them and convert them. In order to avoid this extreme humiliation and loss of dignity the women would voluntarily jump into the burning pyre of their husbands killed by the Mughals. Any Google search will talk about how Akbar wanted to abolish Sati, because history has been written by the invaders and their stooges. While there are good and bad people in every era and every race, we must help our children get over this cancer of glorifying our invaders who caused tremendous damage to our ancestors. After saying this, I will draw from some research I did on Sati:

Sati is one of the favourite topics among Hindu bashers, a question which we have all faced . But what is the truth behind this propaganda to defame Hindu society.

Here is an analysis of some facts of Sati practise.......

SATI PRATHA

First let us look at The Mahabharata and see the reality of death of Madri wife of Pandu.

Pandu had another wife Kunti, why didn't she die? There are hundreds of characters of Mahabharata who died in the battle. Why didn't their wives die? Madri died because she felt guilty of causing her husband's death by going against a curse and consummating their marriage.

How can you generalise things using a singled-out example?

In Ramayana when Dasaratha died none of his three wives go into his pyre.

There is not even a single case of widow burning in our scriptures and itihasas.

The tradition of widows burning themselves in the fire gained prominence from 11th -16th century AD, when hordes of Islamic invaders attacked India from North-west Khyber Pass. Thus, to save themselves from becoming victim of barbarians like Alauddin Khilji, Hindu women started sacrificing their lives by committing **Jauhar**, the term used when women were forced to commit such suicides when they were surrounded by invaders as the last resort, known as **'Death over Dishonour'**.

Sati Pratha is one among the most favourite topic discussed by Hindu-bashers. There are special groups working on intellectual platforms whose duty is to dishonour Hindus as one who oppress Women-hood their equality and rights. These groups do not talk of the archaic practices being followed in other religions till date but speak ill of our Dharma alone. They judge an outdated, extinct and almost forgotten ill practice of Sati Pratha in the name of Human Rights just to belittle and defame Sanatana Dharma.

Origin of Sati Pratha is wrongly attributed to Vedas. This is a big misconception. In reality Sati Pratha is nowhere mentioned in Hindu scriptures. There is no advice of forceful widow burning in Vedas. This confusion was created in Middle Ages by ignorant commentators of Vedas.

Atharvaveda 18.3.1 is mostly quoted as Vedic Mantra which supports Sati Pratha.

This mantra is interpreted as

Choosing her husband's world, O man, this woman lays herself down beside thy lifeless body. Preserving faithfully the ancient custom. Bestow upon here both wealth and offspring. [Translation by Griffith]

In this Mantra the word 'Choosing her husband's world' is often interpreted as Wife is advised to join the Dead Husband in afterlife in next world. So, she must burn herself in funeral pyre of her husband.

The Correct interpretation of this Mantra is

This Women have chosen her Husband's world earlier. Today she is sitting beside your dead body. Now Bestow upon here both wealth and offspring for rest of her life to continue her afterlife in this world.

Thus, this mantra speaks about continuation of worldly affairs by Women in this world after her husband's death.

In the very next Mantra of Atharvaveda 18.3.2 the same advice is attested by the authority of the Vedas. It says...

Rise, come unto the world of life, O woman: come, he is lifeless

by whose side thou liest.

Wife hood with this thy husband was thy portion who took thy

hand and wooed thee as a lover. [Translation by Griffith]

This Mantra clearly speaks to Women to rise besides the dead body of her husband and start worldly affairs in this living world.

Evidence from Rigveda 10:18:8

The Rigveda contains a famous passage mentioning Sati and preventing it. To a widow who is with her husband on his funeral pyre, the text says: rise up, abandon this dead man and re-join the living.

This misinterpretation of Vedic Mantras was done in the Middle Ages by an ignorant class of priests.

The fraud related to interpretation of Rigveda 10.18.7 was exposed by none other than Maxmuller. In this mantra, widowed women as was advised to go ahead (Agre) in her life rather than go in funeral pyre (Agne means fire) after her husband's death. The word Agre was mis-interpreted as Agni. In Mahabharata Madri burned herself to death not due to custom of Sati Pratha but due to regret. She felt that it was her who was responsible for death of her husband Pandu. There is no evidence of Women performing Sati Pratha in Mahabharata post war whose husbands were killed in the Great War. So when a practice was not there way back in the Dvapara Yuga more than 8 Lakh years ago (Or in the period the Mahabharata war happened closer to Kaliyuga, which itself was 5000 years ago). in our most revered Itihasa like Mahabharata, how can it be a part of the Hindu Custom? It wasn't even there in the Ramayana also which was in the 2nd Yuga or Treta Yuga which is approximately 20 Lakh years ago!

Thus, it is proved that Vedas never supported Sati Pratha. Its merely a palpable falsification of a Vedic Hymn which forcibly killed thousands of innocent widows. This ill practice prevailed in the Middle Ages only.

Vedas advise a widow to return from her Husband's corpse and live a happy life.

When Sati did become a baseless ritual, it was rightly abolished as a social evil thanks to the efforts of Raja Ram Mohan Roy and we have moved on, and our women have greatly progressed since.

A big misconception is that the Origin of Sati Pratha is being attributed to Vedas by historians who have a sole objective of brandishing old religions like Hinduism as barbaric while completely ignoring the atrocities against women in other religions – specifically the Abrahamic religions which have a history of burning women in the name of witchcraft for centuries in Europe, and another treating women as second-rate citizens with practices like Triple Talak, Halala, Polygamy (Practiced till date in the modern world) and female genital mutilation. I do not wish to brandish any religion as bad, as that is not how we function, but I would like to state very clearly and loudly that Sanatana Dharma is NOT anti-women whatsoever. I will not cast aspersions or speak ill against any religion and let them practice their faith and I understand that many Muslim women have no problems with these practices themselves so why should we talk ill of them? We do not judge them as per the true tenets of Sanatana Dharma, but at the same time let us not allow them to tarnish our faith and make our (Hindu) girls and women feel that their religion (Hinduism) is inferior – because the truth is it is NOT! We must never tolerate this narrative as it gives our children an inferiority complex thinking other religions are superior to ours because of wrong narrative. Today our children especially in cities feel conscious of wearing the bindi, tilak, Namam or Vibhuti because they don't think our religion is cool and it is backward – the narrative setting starts at home and we are losing this at the family level, because we don't understand the depth and beauty of our religion and are failing to instil a rightful pride about our religion in the minds of our children! I want your daughters to be safe and lead a dharmic life with a dharmic partner. I pray for your daughter(s) and all Hindu girls; I pray to my Guru and the Almighty to keep my daughter and all your daughters in the right Dharmic path when they choose their life partner. We can only guide them and lead by example, the rest is their soul journey, and we can only pray that they get good Dharmic life partners and have a safe, enjoyable life while upholding the core values of Sanatana Dharma. Mind you ALL religions including ours have had some people do a lot of nasty things in the past but let me tell you that Sati the horrible practice that was never in our Vedas or scriptures, has long been banned and we have moved very far from those days, while some religions refuse to move on and do not give women their rights as equal citizens.

Another important aspect we must understand and tell our children is that A MARRIED MAN LOSES HIS RIGHT TO DO MANY RITUALS, RITES AND CEREMONIES WHEN HIS WIFE PASSES AWAY! Does this not show us the high importance of a woman in the atmic upliftment of a man during his Grihastashrama (Married life)?

Now let me narrate a few stories of great Hindu Women that we have to learn about and tell our children:

Chalukya Queen Rani Naiki Devi

We hear stories about the bravery of kings again and again. However, our queens and princesses have never shied away from displaying their heroism and gallantry in order to stand for our country and culture. In search of India's richness and splendour, several foreign countries ventured to gaze up to the land of India. Thousands of valiant sons and daughters of this land responded appropriately to all foreign powers' invasion attempts.

However, the amount of information the laymen have about heroic men in India doesn't match that of brave women. It is critical that we understand and appreciate the contributions of women to our country and society. Be it Queen Velu Nachiyar of the South, Queen Abbakka, or the queen of Jhansi, who fought against the British, we know much about them but there are many who still don't find their place in history textbooks and movies or TV serials.

Here we will explore the tale of a queen who not only displayed otherworldly bravery in forcing Islamic invader Mohammad Ghori to flee but also exhibited remarkable benevolence in sparing his life. Naiki Devi, a queen from Gujarat, not only oversaw the affairs of the empire but also ended up fighting against external invaders.

Who was Rani Naiki Devi?

Rani Naiki Devi was the daughter of Mahamandaleshwar Parmadi, the king of Kadamba. Naiki Devi possessed a wide range of abilities, including horse riding, archery, combat skills, and weapon-wielding. Raja Ajaypal, the Solanki ruler of Gujarat (also known as the Chalukyas), married her. Raja Ajay Pal's reign was short-lived since he died only four years after ascending to the throne. Mulraj II, the son of Naiki Devi and King Ajay Pal, was installed on the throne, but Rani Naiki Devi remained to govern the empire as Raj Mata.

Aspirations of Muhammad Ghori

Muhammad Ghori invaded India between 1175 CE and 1206 CE, capturing Multan (1175), Punjab (1179), Peshawar (1180), Sialkot (1185), and finally Delhi (1192). After capturing Multan in 1175, Muhammad Ghori planned to strike India in search of wealth. Soon after, he led a major army march to Uch in Pakistan's Punjab province's southernmost district. From there, he was able to traverse the desert and begin his journey towards Anhilwara (capital of Chalukyan Kingdom). At the time, Gujarat and Rajasthan were part of the Chalukyan kingdom.

Ghori was obviously confident that the Chalukyas were susceptible to invasion since they lacked a monarch. Because he had a significantly greater army at his disposal, he considered the Hindu queen as weak and easily conquered.

When Rani Naiki Devi learned that Ghori planned to invade her by crossing the desert and landing in her capital city of Anhilwara, she appealed to nearly all neighboring Kingdoms for help in preventing the invasion and safeguarding the kingdom. She did get help from Chalukyan nobles including the leaders of the Naddula Chahamana, Jalor Chahamana, and Arbuda Paramara clans.

The Battle of Kayadara (1178): Ghori Vs Rani Naiki Devi

Naiki Devi realized that her preparations were insufficient to defeat Mohammad Ghori. So, she devised a battle strategy that would benefit her soldiers. She picked Gadarghatta, a rugged region in the slopes of present-day Mount Abu, as the battlefield. This was in the vicinity of Kasahrada village. This location is in the Sirohi district of modern-day Rajasthan.

She picked the terrains because she knew Ghori's army was full of experienced warriors, including steppe nomads who were outstanding archers and superior armored cavalry. Ghori and his warriors, in addition to having a technological edge, were motivated by religious enthusiasm and were passionate about eliminating non-Muslims and transforming the entire territory into an Islamic land.

Ghori's army was unfamiliar with the narrow hill passes of Gadaraghatta, giving Naiki Devi and her allies a significant advantage and balancing the odds in a superb manoeuvre. As a result, when Ghori and his army came, she rode into combat with her son on her lap, leading her troops.

The rest is all history now. The small Chalukyan army and its troop of war elephants routed the invading force, which had previously defeated Multan's formidable sultans. The Rajput war elephants were armored and lined up like mountainside steel. They crushed the morale of Ghori's seasoned armored cavalry.

Ghori's performance in the battle was a colossal failure. He fled the battlefield with a few of his men to save his life.

His pride had been crushed, and he never attempted to conquer Gujarat again. Instead, he turned his attention to the more susceptible Punjab, intending to penetrate north India through the Khyber Pass.

Kittur Rani Chennamma

Have you heard of the Doctrine of Lapse during the British Rule of India? It was a controversial policy of the British Rule to dismantle the Kings and Queens of Bharath. Nobody taught us who all became a victim of this. One such brave Rani was Kittur Rani Chennamma. Chennamma was born in the year 1778 in a village called Kakati, which is in the present Belagavi District of Karnataka. She belonged to the Lingayat community and received training in horse riding, sword fighting and archery from a young age. Now if we Hindus were against women would this be the case so many centuries ago? She married Mallasarja Desai who was the King of Kittur at that time. After a few years of their marriage her husband passed away. Unfortunately, her only son died soon after that. Now, as the queen of Kittur, Rani Chennamma adopted her relative's son Shivalingappa with the objective of making him the heir of the Kittur Kingdom. However, the British East India Company objected to the adoption and ordered Shivalingappa to be exiled from the Kingdom, as part of the Doctrine of Lapse Policy. As per the policy adopted children of Rajas and Ranis could not be successors and if a King and/or Queen did not have a natural legal heir the entire Kingdom would vest and become the property of the British Empire. The British collector ordered Rani Chennamma to surrender her Kingdom and territory to the British Empire, assuming she would fall in line easily. However, the courageous Kittur Rani Chennamma refused to comply to the orders. This refusal led to the first battle between Kittur and the British. Kittur forces were well prepared and fought bravely and the British suffered heavy losses during this battle. The British collector was killed, and two British officers were also taken as hostages by Rani Chennamma's forces. To avoid further bloodshed and war Rani Chennamma negotiated with the British and released the two hostages on the condition that the war would no longer continue. As expected from the power hungry anti dharmic British, they betrayed their agreement with her and waged another war with much larger forces. Rani Chennamma fought the second battle fiercely. For 12 days Rani Chennamma leading from the front along with her forces relentlessly defended Kittur. But once again the Rani was tricked by the British, who made two Indian soldiers of Kittur betray their queen (We have many enemies and traitors within our country even today, wishing for the breaking up and disintegration of our great country and dharmic civilization). These soldiers mixed mud and cow dung in the gun powder used for the canons.

This betrayal made Kittur Rani Chennama lose the battle and the British then imprisoned her for life. The Rani took her last breath in 1829 in prison in the Bhailhongal Fort. The Dharmic woman she was, even in her last few days she spent her time reading Vedic texts and leading a pious life performing Pujas. Today, many of us are even scared to voice our Dharmic thoughts when atrocities and adharma happens, on social media for the want of social acceptance thinking we have to fit in. We should get inspired by the great men and women who fought invaders fearlessly and preserved our culture, traditions and kept the flame of Sanatana Dharma burning bright, and always speak and do what is Dharmic.

RAJMATA RANI AHILYABAI HOLKAR

Rajmata Ahilyabai Holkar was a Holkar Queen of the Malwa Kingdom. Ahilyabai was born on 31st May 1725 in the village of Chaundi, in the present-day Ahmednagar district in Maharashtra.

She was a brave warrior and an excellent archer, who led the army many times to protect her kingdom.

She respected art, music, literature, sculpture, poetry and her court was always open for artists.

Her capital was known for its distinct craftsmen, sculptors and artists who were paid handsomely for their work and kept in high regards by the queen.

She also moved on to establishing a textile industry in the city. She developed Indore into a big and flourished city.

During her reign, the crime rate greatly dropped as she encouraged poor people to get involved in trade or farming. She employed forest tribes to be the protectors of the travelling merchants.

She was philanthropic and provided her people proper infrastructure by properly utilising tax money.

She helped widows in retaining their husband's property so that they can live their lives independently and with honour.

Most of the developments and charity were done by her personal fund which was estimated to be Rs. 16 crores at that time.

During her pilgrimages all over the country, she was appalled by seeing conditions of temples, Ghats and Dharmashalas. She generously donated for upliftment of these holy places.

Famous **Somnath Temple** of Gujarat was reconstructed by her after it was looted and destroyed by Mohammad Ghaznavi.

Kashi Vishvanath Temple of Varanasi and **Vishnupad Temple** in Gaya, Bihar was reconstructed by her. Most of the Ghats near the banks of Ganga in Varanasi were constructed during her reign.

She helped to rebuild temples at **Srinagar, Haridwar, Kedarnath, Badrinath, Rishikesh, Prayaga, Varanasi, Naimisharanya, Rameshwaram, Somnath, Nasik, Omkareshvar, Mahabaleshwar, Pune, Indore, Srisailam, Udipi, Gokarna etc.**

Every holy pilgrimage place in India had a contribution, in one way or another, from Rani Ahilyabai Holkar.

Ahilyabai never issued capital punishment. She took a personal oath from the prisoners & released them.

A prisoner who promised not to commit misdeeds again was released. Many such prisoners adopted an honest life and this generosity showed results.

When Rani Ahilyabai Holkar held court for justice, she always had a Shivling made of clay in her hands.

In memory of this great female ruler, the Government of India issued commemorative stamps in 1966.

Rani Ahilya Bai Holkar was the only public figure who has been conferred with the title of Devi.

Last but not the least

The Great Rani Lakshmibai

Lakshmibai was the queen of Maratha princely state of Jhansi in Uttar Pradesh, India.

Lakshmibai, Jhansi ki Rani was the queen of Maratha princely state of Jhansi in Uttar Pradesh, India. Lakshmibai actively participated in the 1857 rebellion against the British colonial government.

Rani Lakshmibai was born as Manikarnika Tambe on November 19, 1828, in a Marathi Karhade Brahmin family to Moropant Tambe (Father) and Bhagirathi Sapre (Mother). Lakshmibai's mother died when she was four years old. Her father worked for Peshwa Baji Rao II of Bithoor district.

Rani Lakshmibai was educated at home and could read and write. She was also trained for shooting, horsemanship, fencing and mallakhamba. She had three horses-- Sarangi, Pavan and Badal.

In May 1852, Manikarnika was married to Gangadhar Rao Newalkar (Maharaja of Jhansi) and was later named as Lakshmibai as per the traditions. In 1851, Lakshmibai gave birth to her son Damodar Rao who died after 4 months. The couple later adopted Gangadhar Rao's cousin, who was renamed, Damodar Rao. The procedure of adaption was carried out in the presence of a British officer. A letter was handed to the officer from the Maharaja with the instructions that the adopted child should be given due respect and Jhansi should be given to Lakshmibai for her entire lifetime.

However, in November 1853, after the death of Maharaja, British East India Company, applied Doctrine of Lapse, under the Governor-General Lord Dalhousie. Under this policy, Damodar Rao's claim to the throne was rejected as he was adopted son of Maharaja and Rani. In March 1854, Lakshmibai was given Rs. 60,000 as annual pension and was asked to leave the palace.

Rani Lakshmibai: The 1857 Rebellion

On May 10, 1857, the Indian Rebellion started in Meerut. When this news reached Jhansi, Lakshmibai increased her protection and conducted a Haldi Kumkum ceremony to convince her people that the British were cowards and there's no need to fear them.

In June 1857, the 12th Bengal Native Infantry seized the Star Fort of Jhansi and persuaded British to lay their arms and promised no harm to them, but the Infantry broke their word and massacred the British officers.

Sepoys who believed it was Lakshmi bai who had betrayed them, threatened Lakshmibai to blow up the palace, obtained huge money from Jhansi and left the place after 4 days of this incident.

Orchia and Datia kingdoms tried to invade and divide Jhansi amongst them. Lakshmibai appealed the British government for help but received no reply as the British officials believed that she was responsible for the massacre.

On March 23, 1858, Sir Hugh Rose, the commanding officer of the British forces demanded Rani to surrender the city and warned that if she refused, the city will be destroyed. To this, Lakshmibai refused and proclaimed, 'We fight for independence. In the words of Lord Krishna, we will if we are victorious, enjoy the fruits of victory, if defeated and killed on the field of battle, we shall surely earn eternal glory and salvation.'

On March 24, 1858, the British forces bombarded Jhansi. The defenders of Jhansi sent an appeal to Lakshmibai›s childhood friend Tatya Tope. Tatya Tope responded to this request and sent more than 20,000 soldiers to fight against the British Army. However, the soldiers failed to relieve Jhansi. As the destruction continued, Rani Lakshmibai with her son escaped from the fort on her horse Badal. Badal died but the two of them survived.

During this time, she was escorted by her guards- Khuda Bakhsh Basharat Ali (commandant), Gulam Gaus Khan, Dost Khan, Lala Bhau Bakshi, Moti Bai, Sunder-Mundar, Kashi Bai, Deewan Raghunath Singh and Deewan Jawahar Singh. She left to Kapli secretly with a handful of guards and joined the additional rebel forces, including Tatya Tope. On May 22, 1858, British forces attacked Kapli and Lakshmibai was defeated.

Rani Lakshmibai, Tatya Tope and Rao Sahib fled from Kapli to Gwalior. The three of them joined the Indian forced defending the city. They wanted to occupy the Gwalior Fort due to its strategic importance. The rebel forces occupied the city without facing any opposition and proclaimed Nana Sahib as Peshwa of Maratha dominion and Rao Sahib as his governor. Lakshmibai was not able to persuade other rebel leaders to defend the force and on June 16, 1858, British forces made a successful attack on Gwalior.

On June 17, in Kotah-ki-Serai near the Phool Bagh of Gwalior, the British forces charged the Indian forces commanded by Rani Lakshmibai. The British Army killed 5,000 Indian soldiers. Rani Lakshmibai was unhorsed and was wounded. There are two views on her death: Some people say that she was bleeding on the roadside and upon recognising the soldier, fired at him. She was dispatched with his carbine. However, another view is that she was dressed as a cavalry leader and was badly wounded. Rani did not want the British forces to capture her body and told hermit to burn it. Rani Lakshmibai died on June 18, 1858.

In addition to the above great women, we had some amazing women Rishis (Rishikas) who were truly realized souls. To name a few, Yami. Sarasvati, Maitreyi, Gargi, Lopamudra, Madalsa, Urvashi, Anushaya. Koushitaki, Paulomi, Indrani, Visvabhara, Gosa, Sikhata, Sulabha, Apala, Angirasi and many many more.

CHAPTER 18

WHY ARE ALL THE MAJOR SHIVA TEMPLES IN INDIA ALMOST IN A PERFECT STRAIGHT LINE?

This chapter has been taken almost verbatim from Arvind Bhagwat's post on Medium as I found it very well-researched with references (All references have been added to references section).

Yes, many ancient Lord **Siva temples** from **Kedarnath** till **Rameswaram** are aligned in a geographic **straight line** around **79° E 41'54" Longitude**. This is a geographic mystery for many till date since these temples were built during a time when there was no GPS (satellite and technology) and also instruments that could measure the exact longitude and latitude. If this is a fact, then how did this happen and how did this ancient Indian civilization construct temples in such a prefect straight line?

Here is secret behind this sacred mystery:

79th meridian east is ancient **Madyarekha** of India based on **Sumeru** alignment towards **North Pole star** that are primarily used for **Hindu temple construction.**

The meridian 79° east of Greenwich is a line of longitude that extends from the North Pole across the Arctic Ocean, Asia, the Indian Ocean, the Southern Ocean, and Antarctica to the South Pole. The 79th meridian east forms a great circle with the 101st meridian west.

From Pole to Pole

Starting at the North Pole and heading south to the South Pole, the 79th meridian east passes through:

Co-ordinates	Country, territory or sea	Notes
90°0′N 79°0′E	Arctic Ocean	
81°7′N 79°0′E	Kara Sea	Passing just west of Ushakov Island, Krasnoyarsk Krai, Russia Passing just west of Uyedineniya Island, Krasnoyarsk Krai, Russia
73°15′N 79°0′E	Russia	Krasnoyarsk Krai — Nosok Island
73°14′N 79°0′E	Kara Sea	

73°1′N 79°0′E	Russia	Krasnoyarsk Krai — Sibiryakov Island
72°44′N 79°0′E	Kara Sea	Yenisei Gulf
72°22′N 79°0′E	Russia	Yamalo-Nenets Autonomous Okrug Krasnoyarsk Krai — from 69°53′N 79°0′E Yamalo-Nenets Autonomous Okrug — from 69°50′N 79°0′E Khanty-Mansi Autonomous Okrug — from 62°36′N 79°0′E Tomsk Oblast — from 60°48′N 79°0′E Novosibirsk Oblast — from 57°2′N 79°0′E Altai Krai — from 53°40′N 79°0′E
52°7′N 79°0′E	Kazakhstan	Passing through Lake Balkhash
42°47′N 79°0′E	Kyrgyzstan	
41°39′N 79°0′E	People's Republic of China	Xinjiang
35°55′N 79°0′E	Aksai Chin	Disputed between India and People's Republic of China

34°1'N 79°0'E	People's Republic of China	Tibet
33°48'N 79°0'E	Aksai Chin	Disputed between India and People's Republic of China
33°36'N 79°0'E	People's Republic of China	Tibet
33°20'N 79°0'E	India	Ladakh
32°22'N 79°0'E	People's Republic of China	Tibet
31°20'N 79°0'E	Aksai Chin	Disputed between India and People's Republic of China
31°3'N 79°0'E	India	Uttarakhand Uttar Pradesh — from 29°7'N 79°0'E Madhya Pradesh — from 26°35'N 79°0'E Uttar Pradesh — from 26°12'N 79°0'E Madhya Pradesh — from 25°17'N 79°0'E Maharashtra — from 21°36'N 79°0'E, passing 9km west of Nagpur Telangana — from 19°33'N 79°0'E

		Andhra Pradesh — from 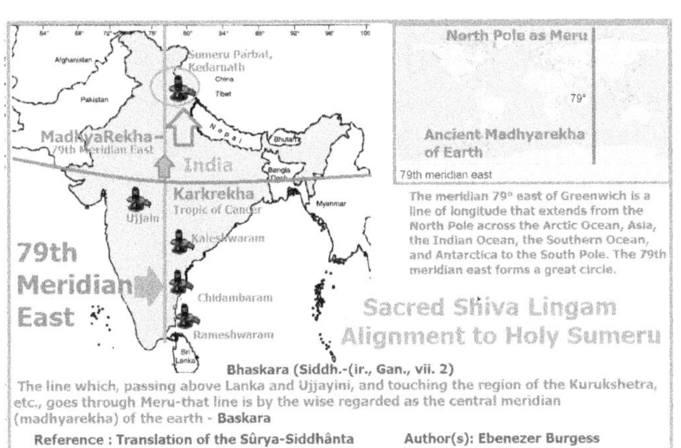**16°14′N 79°0′E** **Tamil Nadu — from** **13°5′N 79°0′E** **Andhra Pradesh — from** **13°3′N 79°0′E** **Tamil Nadu — from** **13°2′N 79°0′E**
9°42′N 79°0′E	**Indian Ocean**	**Palk Strait**
9°21′N 79°0′E	**India**	**Tamil Nadu**
9°16′N 79°0′E	**Indian Ocean**	
60°0′S 79°0′E	**Southern Ocean**	
68°17′S 79°0′E	**Antarctica**	**Australian Antarctic Territory, claimed by Australia**

VārāhaMihira **who was the most famous Indian astronomer from ancient times identified North Pole as the location of** Holy Meru **in his work** Pancha-Siddhāntikā **and same goes with the ancient Hindu astronomical text known as the Suryasiddhanta, locates** Meru **as the** 'Navel of the Earth'.

Below is mention of Madhyarekha by Bhaskara and why it is sacred to align to Meru.

लम्बज्यागुणितो भवेत् कुपरिधिः स्पष्टत्रिभज्याहृतो
यद्वा द्वादशसंगुणः स विषुवत्कर्णेन भक्तः स्फुटः ।
यल्लङ्कोज्जयिनीपुरोपरि कुरुक्षेत्रादिदेशान् स्पृशत्
सूत्रं मेरुगतं बुधैर्निगदिता सा मध्यरेखा भुवः॥२॥

As per current local Hindu cosmogony, **SUMERU PARBAT(6351m)** is present **Kedārnāth mountain** in the **Garhwal district** of **Uttaranchal, India** and below is Shiva Temples and Lingam alignment to Holy Sumeru. Constructing Shiva temples or Vishnu Temples along the **Madhyamrekha** have mythological significance. Ancient Puranas explains the significance and origin of Lingam along this Meridian.

Below are most ancient **Shiva temples** in India that are **perfectly aligned in straight line — 79° Meridian East**

- **Kedarnath — 79.066900° E**
- **Kalpeshwar — 79.449108° E**
- **Rudranath — 79.318445° E**
- **Madhya Maheshwar — 79.221632° E**
- **Baijnath Dham — 79.615734° E**
- **Kaleshwaram, Telangana — 79.904528° E**
- **Mallikarjun Jyotirling, AP — 78.868031° E**
- **Kalahasti, AP — 79.698279° E**
- **Kanchipuram, Tamil Nadu — 79.696243° E**
- **Thiruvannamalai, Tamil Nadu — 79.066688° E**
- **Chidambaram, Tamil Nadu — 79.693521° E**
- **Thiruvanakoil, Tamil Nadu — 78.705673° E**
- **Rameshwaram, Tamil Nadu — 79.317787° E**

Why Sumeru is sacred?

Almost all ancient civilizations considered **circumpolar constellations** such as **Draco/ Shishumara** and **Cygnus** around pole star of Northern night sky as Heaven. These circumpolar constellations never seem to set and they simply rotate around the pole star that basically supported concept of Heaven/God for people of ancient civilizations. It appeared for them as these circumpolar constellations was controlling the movement of all stars and planets around it . In Egyptian terminology, they are referred as **"Indestructibles"**, a perfect destination for the soul of the dead king". Egyptian pyramids are precisely orientated to **North pole star** (**Thuban** during 2800 till 2000 BCE).

In Hindu mythology, these circumpolar constellations are referred as Shisumara planetary system and other stars are also fixed on different sides of the Śhiśumāra planetary system according to the calculations of ancient Vedic astronomers. Even in current world and to concentrate their minds, Vedic sages worship the Śhiśumāra planetary system, which is technically known as the **Kuṇḍalini-cakra.**

Unlike **Hindu cosmology**, even **Jain** and **Buddhist** scriptures mention the **Mount Meru model** as shown above, but **Dhruvaloka** is particularly not mentioned. In **Norse mythology**, they talk about a World Tree that connects Heaven, Earth and Hell just like **Meru.** For Egyptians, **Meru** was something like **Pyramid** that supported God re-birth Myth as the Egyptians believed that the **unmovable area the stars circled** was heaven, the pyramids were built to align north with a single, perfectly aligned vent.

Greeks referred the location of **union** from **earth** to **Heaven(circumpolar constellation)** with structure of **omphalos**, "the navel" of the earth and they localized **Omphalos (Stone of Delphi)** as the central point from which terrestrial life originated in ancient Greek temples of **Delphi** and for **Hinduism**, it is referred as **Linga (Union between Purusha and Prakrati) or Parashiva and Parashakti.**

Below are similarities in Milk offering in ancient Greek and Hindu religious rituals.

Further, in **Hindu rituals**, the symbol with **arms pointing clockwise (卐)** is called **swastika**. If you try to locate the **ancient Ramayana verse** on **'Dhruvam sarve Pradakshinam'** it refers **Dhruvam** as the **pole star** and these **seven sages (Saptarishis)** offer **Pradakshinam**. The word **swastika** is derived from the Sanskrit root **swasti**, which is composed of –

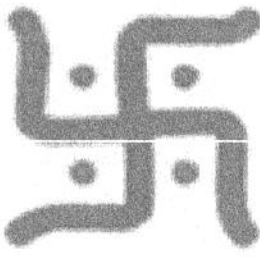

Su (सु) — good, well, auspicious

Asti (अस्ति) — to be or there is.

Most of **Hindu rituals** in which devotees doing **pradaskshina** around God, **pradaskhina** in temples, holy hills, **pradakshina** around **Agni God(Fire)** during **Hindu marriage rituals** have been associated with this cosmology.

Circumambulation is the act of moving around a sacred object or deity.

Circumambulation of temples or deity images is an integral part of Hindu and Buddhist devotional practice (known in Sanskrit as *pradakśiṇā*). It is also present in other religions, including Christianity, Judaism, and Islam.

Even Vibhuti Pada, the third chapter of Patanjali's Yoga Sutras mention the importance of meditating on the pole star.

ध्रुवे तद्गतिज्ञानम् ॥२८॥

dhruve tadgati-jñānam ॥28॥

Explanation : Meditating on the polestar(Dhruva) engenders knowledge (jnana) ||28||

Many famous Buddhist and Hindu temples have been built as symbolic representations of this mountain and several myths have been associated with this holy mountain. If we refer to Hindu Puranas in particular, it describes that Gods reside in the north direction.

Brihadishvara Temple — Tamil Nadu

Please also note that most of Hindu temples are **Meru model** — The famous Brihadeeswara Temple of Tamil Nadu is referred as **"Dakshina Meru"** — the Meru Mountain of the South is a good example. Every Hindu temple is built on a cosmic plan and the roof tower crowning the shrine refers to **Kalasha** (The Purna-Kalasha is considered a symbol of abundance and "source of life" in the Vedas) and temple **Shikara (Gopuram)** represents **Meru** which reaches the ground and extends into the heavens pointing towards the world axis and same goes with the Lingam that were specifically constructed to this cosmogony. It is sacred alignment towards **North Pole star (Kundalini Cakra),** hence they are **constructed in a straight line. The awakening of the Kundalini Chakra in our body gives us God realization and connects Individual Consciousness with the Universal Consciousness.**

Please note that GPS was not available in those times, hence Hindu astronomers have used the ancient Sun Dial to locate the **Pole star** something like the one shown below and you find them in **Ved Shala** in Ujjain.

Ujjain — Ved Shala

The upper planes of the two walls on the sides of the steps in the middle of the instrument are parallel to the axis of the earth. In the direction of the planes the **pole star is visible** were primarily used to align perfectly to the **North Star(Heaven)**. Normally these measurements were done during **Akshaya Tritiya** when the **Sun** is exactly overhead which helped get accurate measurement of **right angle.**

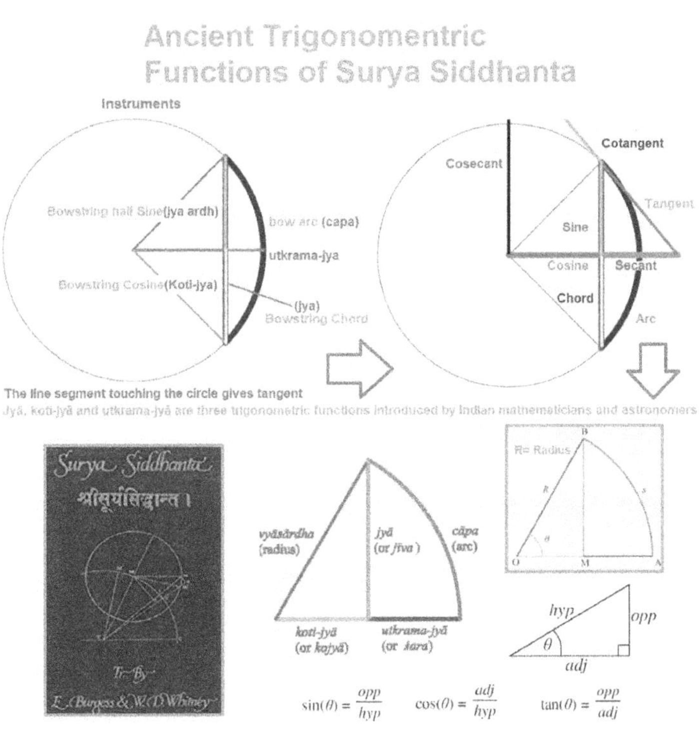

$$\sin(\theta) = \frac{opp}{hyp} \qquad \cos(\theta) = \frac{adj}{hyp} \qquad \tan(\theta) = \frac{opp}{adj}$$

The **Surya Siddhanta** is an ancient Indian text on astronomy and time keeping, an idea that appears much earlier as the field of Jyotisha (Vedanga) of the Vedic period. The text is known for some of earliest known discussion of **sexagesimal fractions** and trigonometric functions. It uses **sine (jya)**, **cosine (kojya or "perpendicular sine")** and **inverse sine (otkram jya)** and also contains the earliest use of the **tangent** and **secant** when discussing the shadow cast by a mid-day sun with Vedic Sundial.

In a similar way, you can locate all the **ancient Sun temples** in **Tropic of Cancer** (ancient **Karkrekha**) like Sun temples of **Orissa, Ujjain, Egypt, Ankor Wat** till **Mexico.** All these ancient structures are perfectly aligned to the North Star and these locations supported in birth of several religions. The day of **Akshaya Tritiya (Vernal Equinox) or when Sun is exactly over head** is auspicious in every religion and you find the scientific reason based on astronomy of past along with earth's axial precession which ancient astronomers were experts at.

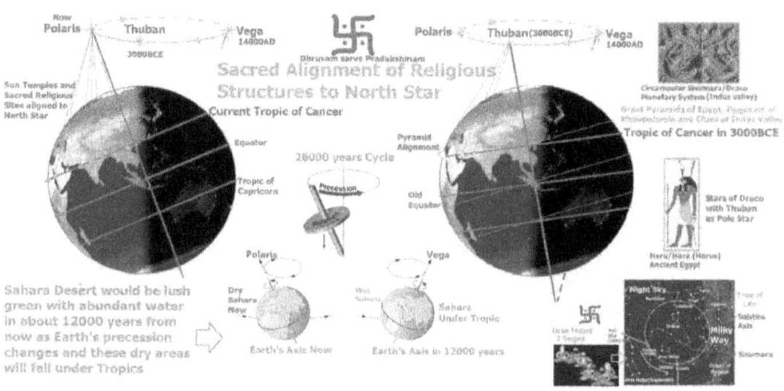

Now do you see the alignment, architecture and significance of our ancient temples? This could not have been an accident but of profound deep thought, science and consecrated structures for our physical, mental, spiritual and emotional well-being. So now do you still think we just worship stones? Can we match this kind of architecture and geo positioning with all the modern science today?

CHAPTER 19

KARMA OR FREE WILL?

From a very young age I have been contemplating on whether we are mere puppets of our past life Karma (Good and bad deeds / actions) or whether we are masters of our destiny. The answer is not a simple yes or no. What I have come to understand from my life experiences and my Gurus is that there is something called Prarabdha Karma (It is Karma that has matured over time that must be dispensed through life experiences in this birth). The Prarabdha karma from our past life is something we just cannot change is what I have come to understand. So come heaven or earth we will go through the good and bad from our good and bad actions of our past birth(s). However, within the purview of that prarabha karma, we have the free will to respond to life situations and do good deeds in this birth that accrue towards our good or bad Karma. So let me try to explain this in simple terms. Some people are born with good health and some people are unfortunately born with health issues. Now let us say you are born with perfect health but decide to eat anything that comes your way and not move or exercise. Your prarabhda karma health-wise was great, but you used your free will to eat and become obese. Now it gets interesting- If your past Karma was so good, you will still lead a healthy happy life despite your bad food habits. On the other hand sometimes we see the healthiest of people pass away early. Covid showed us this at scale. So, with my limited understanding, there is Sanchita Karma (Karmas Heaped together) which is the sum total of all good and bad actions (Karmas) and Prarabdha Karma is one part of it that has matured and come to fruition and has to be experienced in this current physical body / journey. Sanchita Karma are Karmas that might have to be experienced in future but haven't matured and can be marginally changed through good deeds / free will and completely changed by the grace of a realized Guru and the grace of Paramatmma. Finally Agami Karma are your free will actions of the current birth. This is completely up to you and you are the master of your Agami Karma. If one consciously thinks, does and acts in everybody's best interest and always upholds Dharma they can accrue good Karma. However we all make several mistakes daily in thought, word, speech and actions knowingly or unknowingly hurting people etc. as a part of this fast paced competitive world. It is up to us to at least avoid thinking or doing bad for anyone even if we are unable to do good.

CHAPTER 20

IS ASTROLOGY ACCURATE?

Asking if astrology is accurate is like asking if medicine or medical science is accurate. The accuracy of Astrology like any science is dependent on the practitioner. One thing is that our ancients knew that Astronomy was a science and astrology or Jyothisha Shaastra is a branch of astronomy. Our rishis and Gurus realized experientially that celestial bodies by virtue of their positions had an energy impact on us. They then understood that the planetary positions during one's time of birth can predict one's course of life barring interventions by God himself.

My belief in astrology is because of my mother and my aunt Ammu Mami who is like another mother to me. Ammu Mami has been my pillar of strength through my life and has been my rock in my worst days. When I was 13 years old, I was diagnosed with a rare eye condition and doctors told me that I could lose my vision or at best my vision would become extremely bad that I would not be able to go about my day-to-day activities. The only solution they gave me were hard contact lenses or a corneal transplant and even that was not a 100% guaranteed solution, and things could also get worse. I was shattered to say the least as I had my whole life ahead of me and contact lenses were just not suiting my eyes as I had an allergic reaction to them. That is when my mother as she always does called Ammu Mami and told her of the diagnosis. Ammu Mami calmly said, there is nothing wrong in his horoscope, ask him not to do any surgery. She said I will be fine. As a kid, I decided to just follow her words, and I am today almost 44 years old and writing this book. Though I have blurred vision, by God's grace and thanks to a good Astrologer, I have been able to manage with specs. Another instance I wish to quote is in November 2019 when my daughter fell really ill and got hospitalized. Once she was out of hospital, I called Ammu Mami as we were going to travel to Vietnam. I wanted to ask her for a good day to start packing etc. as the previous year we were on our way to Taiwan and my daughter fell ill with bad fever and was hospitalized in Kuala Lumpur our overnight transit destination. We had to cancel our trip and come back. In 2019 when I called her, my aunt (Ammu Mami) told me that the planetary positions are so bad in December 2019 she sees some major natural or man-made calamity could occur starting from the East. She told me something she had never said in all my years of calling her for good/auspicious days. She said, "it's ok if you lose money but please cancel your tickets as it is not advisable to travel especially with kids". While I was shocked, I trusted her and did exactly as she said. It is only later that I realized that Taiwan had warned the WHO about a novel virus that was killing people, in December 2019 itself (Exactly when we were due to travel to Vietnam)! Due to pressure from China WHO never acted on that letter. My aunt didn't know that Covid was about to break out, but her understanding of planetary positions and a deep understanding of astrology made her prevent me from undertaking a travel towards the east when Covid was just starting to spread through flights from Wuhan and air travel in general. I thank God for having a friend, philosopher and guide like Ammu Mami in my life, all thanks to our great Sanatana Dharma. So, our forefathers were unbelievably smart to give us a science like Jyotisha Shastra and the science is as good as its practitioner as with the case in any field of science.

Now let me tell you the story of Varamihira and How Mihira Got the name Varamihira:

This piece about Varamihira has been taken from Shyamsundara Dasa's website as it has been narrated beautifully and accurately.

"Varaha Mihira wrote several important works on Jyotish including but not limited to: Brhat Jataka, Brhat Samhita, Yoga Yatra, Panca Siddhantika (on astronomy) and Prasna Vallabha (apocryphal). We now quote from my book Foundational Topics in Vedic Astrology. Since the abilities of a great savant like Varaha Mihira dwarf those of modern astrologers it also stretches their credulity and thus, they label it mythology."

Shyamasundara Dasa

The importance of Varaha Mihira warrants a brief biographical sketch. The date of Varaha Mihira is controversial, some say circa 100 BC others 500 AD. The date is unimportant for presenting an episode from his traditional biography. The following adumbration from Life of Varaha Mihira, by Suryanarian Rao gives many salient qualities of Varaha Mihira.

Mihira was a Brahmana, the son of Aditya Dasa, from the region of Avanti, near present day Ujjain, in Western India. He was instructed in astrology by his father and was a devout worshipper of Surya Narayana, that is, Krsna who manifests as the Sun. By performing severe austerities to please Surya Narayana, Mihira got blessed with knowledge of ganita, hora, and samhita.

Mihira was one of the Nine Gems, navaratna, in the court of the great king, Vikramaditya of Ujjain. He was greatly honoured by the king for his vast learning and correct predictions. Once, after the birth of the King's son Mihira was asked to make predictions about the prince's future. Going into meditation after studying the chart Mihira " observed that a serious and irremediable danger beset the path of the longevity of the royal child and that he would be killed by a varaha, or boar, on a particular day in a certain month of his 18th year and no human remedies could save the prince from the jaws of death."

Having learnt of this danger to his son from his most reliable of court astrologers, Vikramaditya consulted with Bhatti, his Chief Minister. It was decided that a special palace would be constructed with stupendous walls 80 feet high. Ten thousand elite troops would patrol both inside and outside the property as well as in the palace. Such careful watch was taken of the palace that not even a cat or rat could enter the compound what to speak of a wild boar. Every precaution was taken, and the prince was under constant guard and practically under house arrest, he was not allowed to leave his compound for any reason. In fact, he was ensconced on the seventh floor and not allowed to go to a lower floor. The precautions were so thorough that they boasted that the prince may die but certainly not by the agency of a varaha.

After such security measures were put into place Mihira was asked if he would like to reconsider his former prediction. He emphatically stated that there was nothing that could save the boy. As the date grew near, he was again asked to reconsider, and again gave the same reply. Tension began to mount, not so much for the sake of the boy but for the reputation of Mihira. His detractors thought that Mihira's reputation exceeded his ability, and though the boy might die, the possibility of it being caused by a boar was so remote that Mihira would be publicly disgraced. Even his friends, who had implicit faith in him and knew of his great abilities, had doubts as to how his prediction would be successful, because it was impossible for even a rat to move about undetected in that palace.

On the fateful day Vikramaditya held court. Reports were brought to him every hour on the safety and health of the prince, now 18 years old. All the chief pandits were assembled as well as the navaratnas, the nine greatly learned men, of the King's court. The whole city was waiting for the result of Mihira's prediction. Would it come true or not? The time of death had been fixed at 5:00 PM in the evening. The King, though a great admirer of Mihira, was beginning to doubt Mihira's abilities. With a condescending smile he addressed Mihira, did he still want to maintain his previous prediction that the boy should be killed by a wild boar this afternoon. Did any new calculation possibly change his mind, would the child just die, this was possible, but death by a wild boar would be impossible. The King suggested that Mihira gracefully back down from his former stance, without losing face. The King vowed that if the impossible happened he would give Mihira the highest honour and bestow on him the golden and be-jewelled Royal ensign or emblem, the Varaha, wild boar, that was currently on his crown and transfer it to Mihira's head-dress and that for posterity he would henceforth be given the title Varaha Mihira. Everyone applauded the King.

All eyes focused on Mihira. He rose and gave a speech in which he deprecated his own learning, that unfortunately no great rishis such as Vasishta were present to reverse the karma of the prince. He took a vow that if his prediction failed, he would never practice astrology again, he would never enter the court of the king, and indeed, would leave Ujjain altogether and go deep into the forest to practice Tapasya, austerities, till his last day. But Mihira stated that indeed the death would come true as predicted, there could be no thwarting of fate and the prince would be killed by a boar. He then calmly sat down.

In the afternoon at 2:00 PM the King again convened his court. Senior military commanders came every half hour with news of the prince. He was hale and hearty. Everything was going smoothly. The King had given orders that the guard be on the highest alert and was confident that no harm could befall his son. But Mihiracarya was totally calm, how could this be so, in only a few hours his prediction would be proven wrong, yet he was still placid. Time went on, a half hour after the appointed time of death a guard reported that there was no disturbance in the prince's palace. Mihira calmly told the King that the boy had already died at the appointed time, and they should go see for themselves. Just then another guard came to report that all was still peaceful in the palace. On the way to the palace other guards confirmed that all was quiet and calm at the palace. It was now about 6:00 PM and the King told Mihira that his prediction must have been wrong because nothing at all wrong had been reported, he couldn't believe that his officers were liars.

Mihira replied: " Victorious Monarch! the prince has died at the hour, minute, and second, I have named and none of your watchmen has noticed it. It is a sad event no doubt, but it has happened, and your son is lying dead in a pool of blood, unnoticed by his watchmen and personal companions, and you will see the truth of my prediction. Let us go and examine."

On entering the palace, they noticed on every floor that peace and calm prevailed. On the 7th floor they found a dozen or so of the prince's friends engaged in assorted games such as chess. When the Emperor made inquiries about the prince, they all replied that he had been playing with them a little while ago and that he was quite hale and hearty and that he had just gone out to take some air on the open terrace of the 7th floor.

Mihira said: " The Prince must be lying dead in a pool of blood caused by the injuries of a boar, and if you go to the terrace, you will be shocked to find him dead as predicted by me. This wonderful prediction is not mine. My knowledge is too humble and too limited to make such inconceivable and surprising predictions. I have made all my predictions under the guidance of Surya Narayana. Could such predictions inspired under His grace ever fail?"

They all went to the terrace and saw with horror and sorrow the prince lying dead on a cot in pool of blood. He was disfigured by the iron hooves of the artificial boar-the Royal Emblem-that was attached to the flag staff. Everyone was thrown into simultaneous gloom and ecstasy by the successful prediction. Vikramaditya awarded Mihira with the Royal Emblem and he was hence forth called Varaha Mihira.

The prince's death had transpired in the following way. At about 4:00 PM, the prince, who had been playing with his friends, began to feel a sort of oppression in his chest and giving over his cards to a nearby friend asked him to play in his place. He then rose without complaint and went out to the terrace. A tall flag staff, emblem of Royalty, rose high in the air, it had an artificial boar attached to its top.

As this emblem of royalty was affixed to all important turrets and towers of all the emperor's palaces no one took any notice of them. Near the flag staff was a cot with soft cushions for the prince to take rest whenever he felt fatigued. The prince feeling tired while playing games with his friends came to lay down in the cool air. At 5:00 PM precisely, a very strong gust of wind knocked loose the iron boar. This fell down onto the prince who was lying on his back. The hooves struck severely against his breast and stomach and the tusks struck his head and mouth. The prince lost copious amounts of blood and died immediately. The mattress on the cot absorbed the sound of the crash so no one heard it fall. And as the Prince would often go to the terrace, and as the game was very absorbing, no one noticed the prince's absence.

Spiritual Life the Root of Accurate Predictions

This incident from the life of Varaha Mihira shows the great accuracy that can be attained in astrology if the astrologer is properly trained and performs his spiritual practice and gets the divine blessings. Varaha Mihira lived to be 80 years old, there are many other histories involving him. His son Prithuyashas was also a great astrologer. His son wrote Horasara, an important classic in natal astrology, and Shatpancashika, a text on Prasna. Varaha Mihira was very terse in his own writings, but Horasara is meant to give more explanation of what Varaha Mihira was teaching.

Even after this if you still have doubts about Astrology's evolution from astronomy, think about the Navagraha (Nine Planets) that have been an intrinsic part of all Hindu temples since time immemorial. Not only this, our seers have used their Divya Drishti and understood the impact of these planets on every individual person based on their date, time and place of birth. How did our ancestors know these things and build temples for planets (Grahas) well before any modern scientist knew anything about them? Later, Indian astronomers (Bhaskara, Varahamihra, Aryabhatta) developed mathematical correlations to find distant objects. Varahamihra developed Surya Siddhanta that became the pioneer text of Indian astronomy.

CHAPTER 21

WHY I RESTARTED MY SANDHYA VANDHANAM AFTER A BREAK OF AROUND 10 YEARS?

Till I was in school, post my thread ceremony (Poonal), my mother would make me do my Sandhya Vandhanam (Daily obligatory ritual for a Brahmins, Kshatriyas and Vaishyas that encompasses Yoga, Mantra and Meditation for personal well-being and well-being of all living creatures and people world over). I thank my mother from the bottom of my heart for helping me do this whether I enjoyed it or not. It brought in me a spiritual discipline. Once I went to college, I drifted away and stopped doing this daily practice all together other than once or twice on festival days. Mind you I would always go to an Anjaneya temple in Chennai where I was studying, but just laziness made me stop my obligatory Sandhya Vandhanam. After I finished my education and started working, I started a failed services startup in which we launched a program called Breathing Manager in association with Satyananda Yoga Centre under the Bihar School of Yoga. This was a corporate wellness initiative, and I went to the US and partnered with a company called HeartMath that makes neurofeedback tools to measure heart, breath and brain alignment. While Jeygopalji of Satyananda Yoga Centre taught me the proper way of doing the Nadi Sothanam Pranayama (Which is an intrinsic part of the daily Sandhya Vandhanam), I was shocked to see how the heart, breath and brain activity synchronized using this bio-feedback tool that I was wearing on my ear lobe and seeing the wave pattern on the screen. That is when I realized that no matter what I have to do the Sandhya Vandhanam at least twice a day (It is actually thrikala Sandhya and has to be done 3 times in a day, but doing it in the afternoon is tough because of official responsibilities- however, while witing this book I realized from Mahaperiyava's Hindu Dharma that I can do the noon session 2 hours 24 minutes from sunrise and have started it). I further fine-tuned the Pranayama technique with guidance from HH Krishna Premi Swamigal. Even today I feel bad that in this lifetime I didn't start doing these yogic and meditation practices in the correct way with Gayatri Mantra at a much earlier age, as it would have definitely helped me immensely (I have to thank my mother immensely for pushing me to do my Sandhya Vandanam at least, as she knew it was good for me. Without her insistence I would have been a big zero today in Dharmic matters which have to be learnt through doing and experience. I wasn't told and didn't realize at that point that this was my duty also for the well-being of all creatures earlier). I say this because later I studied the importance of making sure a boy has his thread ceremony by the age of 8 (from conception). The reason is that the calcification of the pineal gland (considered the third eye, the gateway to intuitive and beyond-physical abilities) starts during adolescence. So, a child who starts the proper Sandhya Vandhanam practice young, will have greater intuition, will have better memory, will be more focussed and will have a spark in his eye. We can notice this in brahmachari (celibate) young children in Veda Patashalas even today. We have lost so much wisdom of the Gurukul system to western education which merely prepares us for the material world. Neither me nor Sanatana Dharma itself is against science, technology or education for the material world, but it should not be at the cost of spiritual education (Atma Vidya) which builds character and the ability to control the senses, mind and minimize 6 baser tendencies of the mind and body like lust (Kaama), Anger (Krodha), Greed (Lobha) , Ego (Madha), Jealousy (Matsarya), Attachment (Moha) and a 7th, Alasya (Laziness).

After I started doing my Sandhyavandhanam in the proper manner and meditating while chanting the Gayatri Mantra, till I got Covid, I had much better focus, increased energy and a heightened sense of intuition. After Covid, I was affected physically and mentally, but slowly it is this spiritual practice and the grace of my Guru and God that I am slowly getting back to functioning at least at 50% of what I could. Irrespective of whether you have the practice and custom of thread ceremony, I would urge parents to start off their kids on a Yoga, meditation and shloka (Mantra) discipline early. This is the best gift we can give our children and the world at large.

CHAPTER 22

WHAT WAS THE BRAHMIN VARNA FOR AND WHAT IS THE LEAST A BRAHMIN IN THE MODERN WORLD MUST DO?

I would like to reiterate that I am no authority, in fact I am a failed Brahmin from a Dharmic standpoint and am writing my inferences of Brahmana Dharma after reading speeches of His Holiness Shankaracharya of Kanchi Sr. Chandrashekarendra Saraswati Swami (Mahaperiyava). I do not think I have the right to judge or comment on anyone as I am an imperfect Brahmin (Probably do not even have the right of calling myself a Brahmin as I have not dedicated my life to keep the sound of the Vedas alive for the wellbeing of mankind and all living creatures). I merely do my Sandhya Vandanam as stated earlier also. While I may try, I doubt very much I have the grasping power at this age to learn and recite the Vedas- I sit through sessions my son attends with a Ganapadigal (A person extremely well-versed with the Vedas) and can tell you that it is not at all easy. Children however are able to pick it up like a sponge as their brains are still receptive.

The original role of a Brahmin was plain and simple (but gruelling nonetheless) - to learn through adhyanyana (listening and repeating) from a learned Vedic Guru and recite and keep the sound of the Vedas alive for the well-being of the world and all of mankind and all living creatures. He had to live on the alms of people and not run any business or have any other job. His entire life was to be dedicated to chanting the Vedas, realizing Brahman (Paramatma) within him, while praying for the wellbeing of all people irrespective of their caste, creed, sex, orientation, race, nationality or colour and all living creatures. He had to rise before sunrise in the brahma muhurtham and perform rituals, offer puja to deities and rites for his ancestors every day. The life of a true Brahmin was gruelling with daily rituals starting from early morning before sunrise and ending after sunset. This was for the Agnihotri Brahmins who kept the Aupasana (sacred fire) alive through their lives after their marriage. Their wife would be their dharmic helper in all their Vedic Dharmic duties. Prior to marriage the Brahmachari (Celibate) Brahmin would learn the Vedas staying in a Gurukul with his Guru and his wife, away from his own parents.

Agnihotra is scientific to purify the environment using materials in the sacred fire:

Agnihotra, the simplest form of 'Yajnya/Homa' performed in many countries all over the world. Although it's an ancient fire ritual, it is based on the scientific aspects. It invokes sunrise and sunset timings, when far infrared radiations are produced from the sun, the burning of cow ghee, dried cow dung, unpolished rice in the typical inverted pyramidal shaped copper pot with the chanting of mantras about the Sun (Surya) and fire (Agni). It is found that far infrared radiations of the sun (Wavelengths of 3 μm to 1,000 μm within the infrared range of electromagnetic radiation (light)) and that of Agnihotra resonate to generate a huge amount of vital energy useful for life processes. The fumes and ash of Agnihotra are useful to purify water and air, ameliorate agriculture, reduces the pathogenicity of microorganisms and help to improve the health of living beings. Performing Agnihotra with right timings and ingredients will create conducive atmosphere in the surrounding for the well-being of life.

As researched by Dr. Pranay Abhang and Girish Pathade. You can access the research paper in the following link:

https://papers.ssrn.com/sol3/papers.cfm?abstract_id=3019026#:~:text=Agnihotra%20is%20a%20bio%2Denergy,%2C%20phenols%2C%20formalin%2C%20etc.

So, in a nutshell Brahmins had to do these rituals and the sound of the Veda Mantras they chant and the sacred fire they kept alive through their lives were all as a service to society. Today most of us lead frenzied, frenetic lives with our jobs, businesses and family, that many Brahmins don't even do their obligatory Sandhya Vandhanam. I myself am more of a Vaisya as an entrepreneur which goes squarely against my Brahmana Dharma. Though my mother wanted me to learn the Vedas in the traditional way through adhyayana (listening and repeating) from a learned Vadiyar (Pundit), when I was young, I refused to learn the Vedas not knowing its importance and getting carried away by mundane material education alone, ignoring the all important Atma Vidya and my duty as a Brahmin. Having said this, what can Brahmins do?

As per my Guru's advice, we Brahmins should do our Sandhya Vandhanam in the proper manner thrice a day. If not thrice at least twice a day. We should ensure that our sons have their thread ceremony by 7 years of age (~8 years from conception) of age and we should be their first Guru and teach them the Sandhya Vandhanam and proper way of doing the Pranayama and intonation of the Gayatri Mantra and all mantras and procedures. As per our Dharma Shastras and as per what Mahaperiyava has said, brahmins who fail to do their Sandhya Vandhanam for 3 generations fail to be Brahmins and are just Brahmana Bandus or friends of Brahmins. So, whether we are true Brahmins or not, we should at least be torch bearers of Sanatana Dharma and use our money, and time for uplifting poor Hindus, restoring old temples and contributing our time and money for noble causes like Veda Patashalas, Goshalas and temple khumbabishekams.

As Brahmins we must be able to speak boldly about the beauty of our religion and carry forward the message and ethos to the future generations. We must know in our hearts that we are neither superior nor inferior to anyone. We are hereditary Brahmins but hardly practicing Brahmins and merely Brahmins by birth by virtue of our past birth Karmas. We must use this life to slowly overcome Kama (desire), Krodha (anger), Moha (Attachment), Matsarya (Jealousy), Madha (Ego), Lobha (Greed) and Alasya (Laziness). As Mahaperiyava says in simple words, our lives are comfortable only because our forefathers have done the ordained rituals and have pedalled the cycle for us. We are in a situation where the cycle will travel only for some time before it stops. So, unless we don't get back to our roots and support Dharma and keep the sound of the Vedas alive, our future generations will not enjoy the benefits of our actions. Today, we plan and save material wealth for our children, but Dharmic wealth is much more important for our children and future generations. At this point I digress a bit because I wish to share a beautiful lesson I learnt from a speech by HH Sringeri Shankaracharya Sannidanam Śrī Bhārathī Tīrtha Svāmi. HH Sringeri Shankaracharya HH Sannidanam Śrī Bhārathī Tīrtha Svāmi says it beautifully. He asks us to follow his advise if we really love money. He says there are three types of people. One who is a miser and doesn't enjoy his money or give it to others. One who enjoys his money in this birth but doesn't share it with anyone else and the third who shares his money with those in need. He goes onto say that the first type, the miser is the worst as he neither enjoys his money nor does he help anyone and dies leaving behind his wealth to his legal heirs who will fight over his property and not use it for Dharmic purposes. He says the second is slightly better because at least he enjoys in his current birth what he has, but doesn't accrue any good Karma by helping others. He laughs and says, if you really love money and want to take it with you when you die, be the third type of person and give it away liberally so you carry the Punya with you. He says today people who have money don't give much and those who don't have money don't bless the person who is giving them their money thinking they have a lot so what is the big deal. He concludes saying both are wrong as the rich must give liberally for Dharmic causes and the poor must bless the rich who help them.

At this point I would like to quote verbatim from 2 chapters in Mahaperiyava's Hindu Dharma, where he lashes out at Brahmins as the reason for the decay of Sanatana Dharma and specifically the Varna Dharma. He is such a great soul that he had the authority to speak the harsh truth without mincing any words.

While today the Varna Dharma has decayed to a great extent and politicians merely use it to keep us Hindus divided, we must understand that division of labour was the reason it existed in the past and at that point it worked because there was division of labour and dignity of labour and nobody thought of themselves as superior or inferior. So Mahaperiyava says that the systems were not a vocation for a Varna but a Varna for a Vocation. In the chapter 'Who is Responsible for the Decay of Varna Dharma' he lashes out at Brahmins like myself included, and rightfully so. I quote verbatim from Chapter 6 of Hindu Dharma:

"Politicians and intellectuals alike say that Jati is part of an uncivilized system. Why? Who is responsible for the disintegration of so worthy an arrangement as varna dharma?

These are questions that I raised earlier, and I shall try to answer them. The wrong ideas that have developed about Varna Dharma must be ascribed to the Brahmins themselves. They are indeed responsible for the decay of an age-old system that contributed not only to our Atmic advancement but also the well-being of the nation as well as all of mankind.

The Brahmin relinquished the duties of his birth – the study of the Vedas and performance of the rites laid down in the Vedic tradition. He left his birthplace, the village, for the town. He cropped his hair and started dressing in European style. Giving up the Vedas, he took to the mundane learning of the West. He fell to the lure of jobs offered by his white master and aped him in dress and manners and attitudes. He threw to the winds the noble Dharma he had inherited from the Vedic Seers through his forefathers and abandoned all for a mess of pottage. He was drawn to everything Western; science, lifestyle, entertainment.

The canonical texts have it that the Brahmin must have no love for money, that he must not accumulate wealth. So long as he followed his dharma, as prescribed by the Shastras, and so long as he chanted the Vedas and performed sacrifices, he brought good to the world, and all other Varnas (Castes) respected him and treated him with affection. In fact, they looked upon him as a guide and model.

Others now observed how the Brahmin had changed, how his lifestyle had become different with all its glitter and show and how he went about with all the pretence of having risen on the scale of civilization. The Brahmin had been an ideal for them in all that is noble, but now he strayed from the path of dharma; and following his example they too gave up their traditional vocations that had brought them happiness and contentment and left their native village to settle in towns. Like the Brahmin they became keen to learn English and secure jobs in the government.

For thousands of years the Brahmin had been engaged in Atmic pursuit and intellectual work. In the beginning all his mental faculties were employed for the welfare of society and not in the least for his selfish advancement. Because of this very spirit of self-sacrifice, his intelligence became sharp like a razor constantly kept honed. Now the welfare of society is no longer the goal of his efforts, and his intelligence has naturally dimmed due to his selfishness and interest in things worldly. He had been blessed with a bright intellect and he had the grace of the Lord to carry out duties of his birth. Now, after forsaking his Dharma, it is natural that his intellectual keenness should become blunted.

Due to sheer momentum the bicycle keeps going some distance even after you stop pedalling. Similarly, though the Brahmin seeks knowledge of mundane subjects instead of inner light, he retains yet a little intellectual brightness as a result of the "pedalling" done by his forefathers. It is because of that he has been able to achieve remarkable progress in Western learning also. He has acquired expert knowledge in the practices of the West, in its law, and its industries. Indeed, he has gained such insights into these subjects and mastered their finer points that he can give lessons to the white man himself in them.

A question that arises in this context is how Vedic studies which had not suffered much even during Muslim rule received a severe set-back with the advent of the European. One reason is the impact of the new sciences and the machines that came with the white man. Granted that many a truth was revealed through these sciences – and this was all to the good up to a point. But we must remember that the knowledge of subject per se is one thing and how we use it in practice is another.

The introduction of steam power and electricity made many types of work easier, but it also meant comforts hitherto unthought of to gratify the senses. If you keep pandering to the senses more and more new desires are engendered. This will mean the production of an increasing number of objects of pleasure. The more we try to obtain sensual pleasure, the more we will cause injury to our innermost being. The new pleasures that could be had with scientific development and the introduction of machines were an irresistible lure for the Brahmin as they were to other communities. Another undesirable product of the sciences brought by the white man was rationalism which undermined people's faith in religion and persuaded some to believe that the religious truths that are based on faith and are inwardly experienced are nothing but deception. The man who did not give up his dharmic duties even during Muslim rule now abandoned them for the new-found pleasures and comforts. He dressed more smartly than the Englishman, smoked cigarettes, and even learned to dance like his white master. Those who thus became proficient in the arts of the white man were rewarded with jobs.

Now occurred the biggest tragedy.

Up till now all members of society had their hereditary jobs to do and the did not have to worry about their livelihood. Now, with the example of the Brahmin before them, members of other castes also gave up their traditional occupations for the jobs made available by the British in the banks, railways, collectorates, etc. With the introduction of machinery our handicrafts fell into decay and many of our artisans had to look for other means of livelihood. In the absence of any demarcation in the matter of work and workers, there arose competition for jobs for the first time in the country. It was a disastrous development and it generated jealousy, ill-will, disputes and a host of other evils among people who had hitherto lived in harmony.

Ill feelings developed between Brahmins and non-Brahmins also. How? Brahmins formed only a small percentage of the population. But they were able to occupy top positions in the new order owing to their intelligence, which as I said before, was the "pedalling" done by their forefathers. They excelled in all walks of life – in administration, in academics, in law, in medicine, engineering and so on. The white man made his own calculations about developing animosity between Brahmins and non-Brahmins and realized that by fuelling it he could strengthen his hold on the country. He fabricated the Aryan-Dravidian theory of races, and the seeds of differences were sown among children born of the same mother. It was a design that proved effective in a climate already made unhealthy by rivalry for jobs.

As if to exacerbate this ill-will, the Brahmin took one more disastrous step. On the one hand he gave up the Dharma of his caste and joined hands with the British in condemning the old order by branding it a barbarous one in which one man exploited another. But, on the other hand, though he spoke the language of equality, he kept aloof from other castes thinking himself to be superior to them. If in the past he had not mixed physically with other castes, it did not mean that he had placed himself on a high pedestal. We must remember that there was reason for his not coming into physical contact with the other castes. There had to be differences between the Jatis based on food, work and surroundings. The photographer needs a dark room to develop his films. To shoot a film, on the contrary, powerful lights are needed. Those who work in a factory canteen have to be scrupulously clean; but those who dust machinery wear soiled clothes. This does not mean that the waiter in the canteen is superior to the factory hand who dusts machines. The man who takes the utmost care to keep himself intellectually bright, without any thought of himself, observes fasts, while the soldier, who has to be strong and tough, eats meat.

Why should there be bad feelings between the two, between the Brahmin and the Ksatriya? Does the Brahmin have to come into physical contact with the Ksatriya to prove that he does not bear any ill-will towards him? If he interdined with the Ksatriya he would be tempted to taste meat and such a temptation might eventually drag him into doing things that militate against his own dharmic duty. Each community has its own duties, customs and food habits. If all Jatis mixed together on the pretext of equality without regard to their individual ways of life, all work would suffer and society itself would be plunged in confusion.

It was with definite purpose in view that the village was divided into different quarters; the agraharas (the Brahmin quarter), the agriculturists quarter and so on. Such a division was possible in rural life but not in the new urban way of living. With urbanisation and industrialisation, it became necessary for people belonging to various Jatis to work together on the same shift, sit together in the same canteen to eat the same kind of food. The Brahmins for whom it is obligatory to observe fasts and vows to perform various rites was now seen to be no different from the others. Office and college timings were a hindrance to the carrying out of these rites. So, the Brahmins threw them to the winds. He had so far taken care to perform these rites with the good of others in mind. Like a trustee, he had protected Dharma for the sake of society and made its fruits available to all.

All that belonged to the past. Now the Brahmin came forward proclaiming that all are equal and that he was one with the rest. All the same he became the cause of heartburning among others and – ironically enough – in becoming one with them he also competed with them for jobs! That apart, though he talked of equality, he still thought himself to be superior to others, in spite of the fact that he was not a bit more careful than they about performance of religious duties. Was this not enough to earn him more hatred?

The Brahmin spoiled himself and spoiled others. By abandoning his dharma, he became a bad example to others. Now, after he had divested himself of his dharma, there was nothing to give him distinction, to mark him out from others. **As a matter of fact, even by strictly adhering to his dharma the Brahmin IS NOT ENTITLED TO FEEL SUPERIOR TO OTHERS.** He must always remain humble in the belief that "everyone performs a function in society" and that "I perform mine". If at all others respected him in the past and accorded him a high place in the society it was in consideration of his selfless work, his life of austerity, discipline and purity. Now he has descended to such depths as to merit their most abrasive criticism.

It is my decided opinion that the Brahmin is responsible for the ruin of Hindu society. Some people have found an explanation for it. The Brahmin, if he is to be true to his Dharma, has to spend all his time learning and chanting the Vedas, in performing sacrifices, in preserving the Sastras, etc. What will he do for a living? If he goes in search of money or material, he will not be able to attend to his lifetime mission – and this mission is not accomplished on a part time basis. And if he takes up some work for his livelihood, he is likely to become lax in the pursuit of his dharma. It would be like taking medicine without the necessary diet regimen; the benign power gained by the Brahmin from his Vedic learning will be reduced and there will be a corresponding diminution in the good accruing to mankind from his work.

This is one reason why Brahmins alone are permitted by Sastras to beg for their living. In the past they received help from the kings- grants of lands, for instance – in consideration of the fact that the dharma practiced by them benefited all people. But the Sastras also have it that the Brahmins must not accept more charity than what is needed for their bare sustenance. If they received anything in excess, they would be tempted to seek sensual pleasures and thereby an impediment would be placed on their inner advancement. There is also the danger of their becoming submissive to the donor and of their twisting the sastras to the latter's liking. It was with a full awareness of these dangers that in the old days the Brahmins practiced their dharma under the patronage of Rajas (accepting charity to the minimum and not subjecting themselves to any influence detrimental to their dharma).

The argument of those who have found an excuse for the conduct of latter-day Brahmins goes thus- "Brahmins ceased to receive gifts from rulers after the inception of British rule. How can you expect them to live without any income? Force of circumstances made them take to English education and thereafter to seek jobs with the

Government. It is unjust to find fault with them on that score."

There is possibly some force in this argument, but it does not fully justify the changes that has come over Brahmins. Before the British the Mughals ruled us and before them a succession of sultanates. During these periods a few pandits must have found a place in the darbar. But all other Brahmins adhered to their dharma, did they not, without any support from any ruler? The phenomenon of the Brahmin quarter becoming deserted, the village being ruined, the pathasala (Vedic School) becoming forlorn and the lands (granted to Brahmins) turning into mere certificates is not more than a hundred years old. Did not the Vedic Dharma flourish until a generation ago? (Two generations ago, as I write this, but Periyava spoke about this around 50 years ago roughly).

The Vedic religion prospered in the past not only because of patronage extended to the Brahmins by Hindu rulers. People belonging to all varnas (castes) were anxious that it (The Vadic Religion -Sanatana Dharma) should not become weak and perish. They saw to it that the Brahmin community did not weaken and contributed generously to its upkeep and to the nurturing of the Vedic tradition. Today you see hundreds of Vedic schools deserted. There are few Brahmin boys willing to study the scriptures. Who had raised the funds for the Vedic Institutions? [In Tamil Nadu] the Nattukottai Nagarattars, Komutti Cettis and Vellalas. The work done by Nagarattars for our temples is indeed remarkable. Throughout Tamil Nadu, if they built a temple, they also built a Vedic school along with it in the belief that the Vedas constituted the "root" of the temple. This root, they felt, was essential to the living presence of the deity in the temple and for the puja conducted there. Similarly, the big landowners among the Vellalas made lavish donations to the Vedic schools.

If the Brahmin had not been tempted by the European lifestyle and if he were willing to live austerely according to the dictates of the sastras, other castes would have come forward to help him. It is not that the others deserted him, He himself ran away from his dharma, from his Agrahara, from his village and from the Vedic school because of his new appetite for the life of luxury made possible with the new technology of the West. He forgot his high ideals and paid scant respect to the principle that the body's requirements are not more than what it takes – in physical terms – to help the well-being of the Self. All told the argument that the Brahmin was compelled to abandon his dharma because he was denied his daily bread does not hold water. We cannot but admit that the Brahmin became greedy, that he yearned far more than what he needed for his sustenance.

Let us consider that the Brahmin left his village because he could not feed himself there and came to a city like Madras. But did he find contentment here? What do we see today in actual practice? Suppose a Brahmin receives a salary of Rs. 1000 in Madras today, if he gets a job in Delhi with double the salary, he runs off there. Later, if he were offered $4000 a month in America he would leave his motherland for that country, lured by the prospect of earning a fortune. There, in the United States, he would become totally alienated from his religion, from his dharma, from all his traditions. The Brahmin is willing to do anything, go to any extent, for the sake of money. For instance, he would join the army if there were promise of more income in it. If necessary, he would even take to eating meat and to drinking alcohol. The usual excuse trotted out for the Brahmin deserting his dharma does not wash.

I will go one step further. Let us suppose that, following the import of Western technology, other communities also become averse to observing their respective dharmic traditions. Let us also assume that, with their thinking and feelings influenced by the Aryan-Dravidian theory concocted by the English, these castes decided not to support the Brahmins any longer. Let us further assume that to feed himself (for the sake of a handful of rice) the Brahmin had to leave hearth and home and work in an office somewhere far away from his native village. Were he true to his dharma he would tell himself "I will continue to adhere to my dharma come what may, even at the risk of death". With this resolve he could have made a determined effort to pursue Vedic learning and keep up his traditional practices.

There is no point, however, in suggesting what people belonging to the generation gone by should have done. I would urge the present generation to perform the duties that the past generation neglected to perform. To repeat, you must not forsake your dharma even on pain of death. Are we going to remain deathless? As it is we accumulate money and, worse, suffer humiliation and earn jealousy of others and finally die losing caste by not remaining true to our dharma.

Is it not better then to starve and yet be attached firmly to our dharma so long as there is breath in us? Is not such loyalty to our dharma a matter of pride? Why should we care about how others see us, whether they honour us or speak ill of us? So long as we do not compete with them for jobs, they will have no cause for jealousy or resentment. Let them call us backward or stupid or think that we are not capable of keeping abreast of the times. Are we not now already their butt of ridicule? Let us be true to our dharma in the face of mockery of others, even in the face of death. Is not such a lot preferable to suffering the slings of scorn and criticism earned by forsaking our dharma for the sake of filling our belly? People nowadays die for their motherland; they lay down their lives for their mother tongue. They do not need a big cause like the freedom of the country to be roused to action; they court death, immolate themselves, even for a cause that may seem trivial like the merger of a part of their district in another. Was there any demonstration of faith like this, such willingness to die for a cause or a belief, when the British came here with their lifestyle? At that time did we protect our dharma with courage, in the belief that even death was a small price to pay for it?

The Lord himself has declared in the Gita that it is better to die abiding by one's dharma than prosper through another man's dharma ("nidhanam sreyah"). Brahmins who had seen no reason to change their lifestyle during the long Muslim period of our history changed it during the British rue. Why? New sciences and machinery came with the white man. The motor car and electricity had their own impact on life here. Brahmins were drawn to comforts and conveniences not thought of before. This could be a reason for their change of life, not a justification.

The Brahmin is not to regard his body as a means of enjoyment of sensual pleasure but as an instrument for observance of such rites as are necessary to protect the Vedas – and the Vedas have to be protected for the welfare of mankind. The basic dharma is that to the body of the Brahmin nothing must be added that incites his sensual appetite. It was a fundamental mistake on the part of the Brahmin to have forgotten the spirit of sacrifice that imbues his dharma and become a victim to the pleasure and comforts easily obtained from the new gadgets and instruments. There is pride in adhering to one's dharma even when one is faced with adverse circumstances. Brahmins (during British Rule) committed a grave mistake by not doing so and we are suffering the consequences. See the ill-will in the country today among children of the same mother. We have created suffering for others also. At first Brahmins were denied admission to colleges and refused jobs. Now things have come to such a pass that other communities also suffer the same fate.

All was well so long as man, using his innate resources, lived a simple life without the help of machines. With more and more factories and increasing machine power, life itself has become complicated. The situation today is such that everyone is facing difficulties in getting admission to college or in getting a job.

People ask me "What is the remedy? Do you expect all Brahmins to leave their new lifestyle and return to Vedic learning?" Whether or not I expect them to do so and whether or not such a step seems possible, I must ask them to do so (to return to their Vedic Dharma). Where is the need for a Guru-Pitha or a seat on which an Acarya is installed if I am to keep my mouth shut and watch idly as dharma that is the source of everything is being endangered? Even if it seems not possible (Brahmins returning to the Dharma of their birth) it must be shown to be possible in practice: that is the purpose of the institutions called Mathas. They must harness all their energies towards the attainment of this goal.

During the years of the freedom struggle some people wondered whether the white man would quit because of satyagraha. Many things in this world regarded as not being within the realm of possibility have been shown to be possible. It is not for me to say that this (the return of all Brahmins to the Vedic dharma) is not possible; to take such a view would be contrary to our very Dharma. It is up to you to make it possible in practice or not to make it possible. All I can do is keep reminding you of the message of the Dharmasastras.

Mahaperiyaya goes on to say in the next chapter The Least Brahmins Can Do:

Whether or not the present Hindu society changes and whether or not it can be changed, it is essential to have a class of people whose very life-breath is Vedic learning. I do not speak thus because I am worried about the existence of a caste called Brahmins. Nothing is to be gained if there is such a caste and it serves only its selfish interests. **If a caste called Brahmins must exist, IT MUST BE FOR THE GOOD OF MANKIND.** The purpose of the Vedas, the sound of the Vedas, is the well-being of the world. That is the reason why I feel that, hereafter at least, there ought not be even a single Brahmin who does not chant the Vedas. The only remedy for all the ills of the world, all its troubles, is the return of all Brahmins to the Vedic Dharma.

In this context I should like to tell you the least expected of Brahmins. I am prepared to ignore the fact that they have neither the courage nor the spirit of sacrifice necessary to come back to their dharma. But they can at least make their children take to it. In the next generation there must not be a single Brahmin who is not conversant with the Vedas. You must work for this goal and make sure your sons learn these sacred texts.

If you are averse to making your sons mere Vaidikas (one who is learned in the Vedas who dedicate their lives to chanting the Vedas for the well-being of all of mankind and creatures), and are anxious that they too should lead a life of comfort like you (what you think to be a life of comfort), I am prepared to come one step further down to make the following suggestion. You would not perhaps like your children to take up Vedic learning as a lifelong vocation and would like to give them education on modern lines so as to prepare them for office or factory work or make them doctors, engineers, and so on. I am prepared to go with you so far. But I would ask you to perform the Upanayana of your son when he is eight years old. He must then be put in a Veda class held for one hour in the evening after school hours. He must be taught the Vedas in this manner for ten years.

This is the least Brahmins can do to preserve the Vedic tradition. Arrangements to impart Vedic learning to children must be made in every Brahmin household. I know that there are not enough teachers, a sad reflection on the state of our dharma. Considering this and the likely economic condition of the parents I would suggest that Veda classes may be conducted for all children of a locality or neighbourhood. Children of poor families may be taught on a cooperative basis.

Step by step in this way the boys will be able to memorise the mantra part of the Vedas and also learn the prayoga (process) to conduct rites like Upakarma (Thread ceremony / Changing of thread and Veda Arambam). I speak about "Prayoga", the conduct or procedure of rites, because in the absence of Purohits (priests) in the future everyone should be able to perform Vedic rites himself.

The sound of the Vedas must pervade the world for all time to come. Everyone must sincerely work towards achieving this end. **It is your duty to ensure the good not only of the Brahmin community, not only of all the castes of India, but of all countless creatures of Earth. It is a duty imposed on you by Isvara – it is a divine duty.**

It is important that we perform this duty we owe to the people of the present. But it is equally important that we perform it so as to be saved from committing a crime against future generations. "As it is nobody cares about the Vedas," you are likely to tell me. "Who is going to care for them in the coming years? What purpose is served by all the efforts we take now to keep up their study?" I do not share this view. When the wheel keeps turning, that part of it which is now down has necessarily to come up. Modern civilization with its frenzied pace is bound to have its fall after attaining its peak. We have been carried away by the supposed comforts made possible by advanced technologies. But one day we will realise that they do not give us any feeling of fullness and that we have indeed created only discomforts for ourselves through them.

The example of America is enough to drive home this point. People there are believed to have attained the acme of luxury and yet feel empty within. They are anxious to dispel the disquiet created by modern comforts. Americans who have some degree of awareness have been drawn towards Vedanta, yoga, devotional music and so on. Others want to forget sensual enjoyment somehow. They swallow all kinds of tranquilizers and are immersed in a deep stupor.

This fate may overtake our country also. We are always tempted by the feeling that there is some worldly pleasure yet to be savoured and we know no rest until we have done so. After draining pleasures to the dregs, we will discover the impermanence of it all. That is the moment when we will turn to matters of the Self, to the quest of enduring bliss. If we of this generation create a break in the chain of Vedic study kept up for ages, from generation to generation, we shall be committing the unforgivable crime of denying our descendants the opportunity of learning the Vedas.

"There are so many books dealing with the Vedic mantras and sacrifices, volume after volume produced by Indian and foreign scholars," the suggestion is likely to be made. "Surely the future generations can read them and learn the Vedas thus."

Before I speak about this, I have to answer another important question, a question that goes to the very heart of the Vedic tradition. It is this: "What do you mean by saying the sound of the Vedas protects the world? The mantras are certain sounds expressed in the form of words. These words have meaning from books? Why should there be a class of people specially devoted to chanting the Vedas? If the meaning of the scriptures is to be preserved there is no cause for worry since there are books to serve such a purpose. There is no need for an exclusive caste functioning on a hereditary basis and charged with the duty of preserving these texts. But the question of the meaning of the Vedas apart, why should there be a class of people whose duty it is to chant the Vedas hymns and preserve their sound in the form it has come to us from time immemorial?" This question must be answered." "

The above ends the long part where I have quoted Mahaperiyava from the Book Hindu Dharma. If you

wish to go more in depth on the subject, please do buy a copy of the Hindu Dharma by HH Jagadguru Chandrasekharendra Sarasvati Svami.

Now that you (If you are a Brahmin) and I are feeling miserable about how we have failed in our duties to protect Dharma to varying degrees, I would like to state that all is not lost. Yes, over the last 2 generations Brahmins have gotten carried away by modern education and to a large extent diluted or completely left their dharma. Having said this, today we live in a market economy where all of us are working, managing businesses or in employment (In later chapters in Hindu Dharma Mahaperiyava also kindly states that Brahmins are not a privileged caste because they have to maintain purity of their body and mind and perform rigorous rituals for the well-being of mankind and that hate against them in today's world is not warranted). Today Bala Periyava (His Holiness Jagadguru Vijayendra Saraswati Swamigal) my Guru does not dissuade us from leading comfortable lives and openly says we must embrace technology but without sacrificing our dharma. In the Veda patashalas run by the Kanchi Mutt, children go through Vedic learning and English education affiliated to the CBSE board. Our dharma is scientific, and the sound of the Vedas are extremely important for the well-being of the world because the Vedas hold lofty truths and are an embodiment of the sound of the cosmos which our rishis have discovered through great tapas and penance and passed on from one generation to the next. Now moving to today's world, it is unfortunate that not only are Brahmins bashed, but even Sanatani Hindus of other castes are also abused. It is a sad state that everything that has the words "scientific" is believed even if it comes from big pharma companies that cut corners to make a profit at the cost of our health, but we do not believe in dharmic truths till a foreigner accepts and endorses it. So let us make it very clear that calling all Brahmins scoundrels is like calling all Muslims terrorists. There is absolutely no difference between the two. In fact, it is a very dangerous narrative because it is harming the very Brahmins who are actually upholding our Dharma, the most. The temple priests and Vaideegas who are earning paltry sums of money sometimes as low as Rs. 12000 a year because our temples are under government control (unconstitutionally), are being ostracized and bullied the most. It is our duty to help these people and make sure their future generations don't quit upholding our Dharma out of sheer frustration. As educated Hindus, we really have to do whatever it takes to help and not further this divisive agenda of certain anti-Bharath and anti-dharmic forces that are at play in devious and sinister ways. These forces at play know that eliminating the dharmic Brahmins will weaken Sanatana Dharma itself greatly and hence they vilify Brahmins and make them look like terrorists, which is far far away from the truth in today's adharmic world.

So, as Mahaperiyava says, it is our duty to get back to Vedic learning and get our children to study the Vedas from a knowledgeable Guru after school hours. My son had his Upanayanam when he was 8 and does his Sandhyavandhanam daily. He started learning the Vedas for a few years but due to various factors there was a break but is now restarting. I hope to make some time to learn at least what I can with him – but learning the Vedas is easiest when a child is between 8-17/18 years old (So at my age I don't have too much hope of memorising these complex divine hymns and mantras). It is also our duty to support Veda Patashalas and dharmic causes like temple Khumbabishekam (Reconsecration rituals of temples done every 12 years), preservation of old temples belonging to all castes etc monetarily and with our time and efforts.

So as Brahmins and Bharatiyas what can you do:

1. **Stay in Bharath as far as possible or come back home if you live abroad. If you can't come back, be a cheerleader of your community and Hindus and Hinduism from wherever you live. I have been asking my friends and relatives to come back to India, for very long now.**

2. **Try to buy land in your native place / village. Reclaim the Agraharams we have long forgotten and lost (If possible)**

3. **Support temples of ALL castes (Yes, all Varnas have their own temples and we must support them all. Including all castes and making them feel a part of a larger civilizational cause is more important than ever.). Take your children to village temples like that of Aiyanar and Mariyamman and immerse them in these truths that all Castes have temples that they**

manage so they don't fall prey to wrong anti-brahmin narratives.

4. Do your Sandhyavandhanam thrice daily (Morning, noon and evening) and set an example to your sons to follow. Mahaperiyava has guided us that Madhyanikam (Noon ritual) can be done 2 hours 24 minutes after sunrise (Sangava Kala) if one has to go to office/school and can't do it at Noon (I have personally started doing this recently). Women and Shudras need not do it because, they become inwardly pure by doing their work (Karma Yoga) for their family and society respectively and get the benefits of the Gayatri Mantra from the men of the family doing it. This is not inequality but freeing women of these rigorous ritual duties because they already have a lot of work to do without being bound by rituals. Also, the Vedic mantras are strenuous and meant for the male physiology. With respect to the Shudras, they are neither less nor greater than Brahmins, they are free from these rituals that the other 3 Varnas are duty bound by and achieve their inward purity through their labour – Karma Yoga and gain benefits of the Vedic Mantras chanted by the Brahmins and Gayatri Mantra chanted by Brahmins, Kshatriyas and Vaishyas. So, if we had to do something only for ourselves, we can decide whether to do it or

not. But Brahmins especially are duty-bound to do it for Loka Kshemam or well-being of the women, all Varnas and the world at large, so we cannot be lackadaisical about these duties.

5. Make sure your sons learn the Vedas and do their Sandhya Vandhanam and Gaytri Japam thrice daily. Fathers should set an example by doing at least the Sandhya Vandanam themselves.

6. Make sure your daughters learn slokas and Itihasas and drawing of the traditional Kolam / Rangoli with rice flour. Kolams not only help in the mental and physical health of the woman it also helps feed ants, birds and small creatures. Make them do a small daily Puja by reciting a small shloka and offering food to God 'Neiveidyam' and crows (crows are supposed to be our pitrus-ancestors) and also light an oil lamp at the doorstep of your house and in the Puja room. The Woman of the house (the mother) should make sure they do it so their daughters watch, learn and practice these very important rituals.

7. Make sure your daughters understand the importance of our Hindu symbols like a bindi and sons learn the importance of Vibhuti, Tilak or Namam. The forehead has acupressure points that are activated when we apply these symbols. The prefrontal cortex is activated on

daily application of the symbols on the forehead, while the Vibhuti also tells us that this body eventually becomes ash and keeps us humble.

8. Make sure your daughters and sons learn hygiene aspects of day to day living and the importance of offering food to God, crows /animals and other living creatures before eating daily.

9. Visit temples regularly and donate liberally to the priests directly and to the temple trusts.

10. Perform last rites and ceremonies of your deceased parents and the departed as per the shastras. Perform Amavasya Tarpanam every month and annual Shradham if your parent(s) are no more and you are a son.

11. Donate to temples, especially old temples which are dilapidated.

12. Donate liberally to Veda Patashalas to the best of your capacity

13. Support poor Brahmins who are upholding Dharma.

14. Support ALL poor Hindus monetarily and do annadhanam (provide free food) for the really poor.

15. Celebrate all Hindu festivals and make them an enjoyable family affair for your children. . Make your children enjoy them and know the history and relevance of the festivals. Keep away your phones during the Puja!

16. **DO NOT SPEAK ILL OF YOUR RELIGION EVER. STAY UNITED.**

17. **Make being Dharmic the new cool. Don't be woke - it makes you live a lie and harms your inner self. Sanatana Dharma is the most inclusive you can get so wear it on your sleeve proudly. If you don't respect yourself, you can never truly respect another.**

18. **Support in the modern education of all poor Hindus so they have a good life.**

19. **Visit your Kula Deivam temple at least once a year and make sure the temple is in good shape.**

20. **Put pressure on the Governments to free our temples so they can be managed by the community that it belongs to – get united, use your collective voice on social media and beyond. This is a constitutional right that all our governments so far have gone against. ONLY HINDU TEMPLES ARE UNDER GOVERNMENT CONTROL UNCONSTITUTIONALLY- Religious institutions of other religions are not under Government control. (If temples have been freed from Government control by the time you read this book, congratulations- please make sure it stays this way as funds donated by Hindus should be used for the upliftment of the Hindu society and Dharmic purposes. The Government has other sources from taxes for other general welfare schemes for all citizens.)**

CHAPTER 23

KNOW YOUR HISTORY AND ACKNOWLEDGE IT

Prosperity, Knowledge and economy of Ancient Bharath:

India's prosperity and knowledge from the Vedic age resulted in the Indus Valley Civilization around 3300 BC. From then on to founding phenomenal Universities like The Nalanda University, Bharat was rich, prosperous and highly advanced. Nalanda University was built by Kumaragupta of the Gupta dynasty in the 5th century BC. Prominent rulers of the time, including King Harshavardhana of Kannauj, Pala Rulers, and many scholars patronized Nalanda. According to Angus Maddison the renowned British Historian, India's share of GDP was 33% in 1 CE and declined to a measly 3% after the Mughal and British invasions. Today, if we visit temples like 900-1000 year-old temples Belur, Halebid and the destroyed temples of Hampi or the Big Brihadeeshwarar Temple (Gopuram height of 216 ft!!! the tallest in the world and that too with beautiful symmetrical carvings) Tamil Nadu, we can get a glimpse of Bharat's unbelievable scientific prowess, architecture and knowledge. The ruins of Hampi show us of the advanced scientific prowess of our people during the 15th century when the temple was built by King Devaraya II which was further expanded and enhanced by Krishnadevaraya. The ruins also show us of the sheer barbaric nature and Hindu hatred of the Mughal rulers who broke the noses and destroyed the deities in the temples. Even in our so-called modern world, we do not have architects who can build such marvels and intricate carvings as was done in the so called 'medieval' , 'barbaric' India as some historians with a biased view would like us to believe.

India's share of GDP based on research by Angus Maddison:

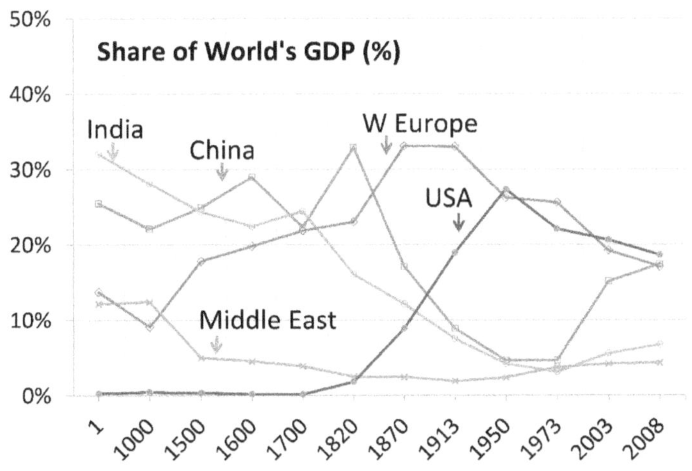

https://en.wikipedia.org/wiki/Angus_Maddison_
statistics_of_the_ten_largest_economies_by_GDP_
(PPP)

We should take our children to temples and key historic sites of India like the cellular jail in Andaman to teach them how our forefathers and freedom fighters suffered during the invasions. We should teach our children of the glorious knowledge of our Vedic Civilization and make them take pride in our culture and heritage while also learning all that today's modern education has to offer.

On a recent trip to Sakleshpur with my parents, my kids and wife, I decided to take a short detour to Belur on our way back to Bangalore. I wanted my kids to see the Belur Chenakeshava Vishnu temple. My kids 6 and 13 were spellbound by the carvings, deities and sheer intricacy of design on whole rocks. Imagine a moving bangle carved on a beautiful Parvati from a single stone? Every pillar of the temple is unique, and each one tells a story. The entire Dasa Avataram or theory of evolution is inscribed and depicted on the walls of the temple. My son was amused to see a teenage boy with a girl with a donkey face, depicting the play of hormones, when a boy will even find a girl who looks like a donkey attractive when he is around 16 years old. This shows that sex education and knowledge of the human physiology, desires and needs were way ahead of most parts of the world. There are sculptures of divine feminine shakti in short skirts and bathrobes (Doesn't this show how open-minded and forward thinking we were as a civilization till we were invaded?). The depiction of the feminine and their powers and skills in archery, their emotions etc are so amazing that I feel sad that we lost a lot of all that during the Mughal and British eras which took us back in more ways than one. Today we are talking about 'women empowerment' from being a human-centric, pro-women modern and affluent land, well before Christ.

A few photos from Belur Chenakeshava temple that I took:

The Barbaric Nature of Invasions:

It is sad that today the educated Hindu, does everything to twist history to make himself look holier than thou. Historic facts state that anywhere over 100 million Hindus were raped, killed and eliminated during the Mughal rule over a 1000-year period. Today the intellectual Hindu says, so what, they became a part of us. How did they become a part of us, was it peacefully or by force? The answer is very clear. Whether we like to acknowledge it or not, with zero hate for any religion or any person currently belonging to any religion, I state that our women were raped, tortured and impregnated by horrible invaders like Aurangzeb. Today, if we state these facts, we are considered communal. How is it communal? Am I asking anybody to hate the present-day Muslims? No. But let us understand that Islamic invasions were brutal and had an agenda to convert or kill the indigenous populations (Hindus and all other indigenous religions). Now, imagine having a road named after Hitler in Israel. The Irony is we still have several roads and localities named after Invaders who came and ethnically cleansed us. The Mughal rule was arguably the biggest genocide of native people that the world has ever seen. So, turning a blind eye to that and acting like it never happened like how our history books cover history, is a shame. Today, unfortunately our biggest enemies are not people of other religions but our own Hindus who lie to cover historic facts and act like they are the only ones who care for people of other faiths. This stems from their basic insecurity, inferiority complex and lack of knowledge of Sanatana Dharma which is the world's oldest religion and most accepting of all religions up to a point that they try to convert us by force or coercion. As Lord Krishna tells Arjuna in the Bhagavad Gita, that upholding Dharma for the well-being of the world is paramount and he must not think before killing his own elders and army of his brothers because they were adharmic forces that would harm humanity if left alive (He asked Arjuna to do his duty with God in mind and no hatred so he doesn't accrue any bad Karma). In the modern day our Kshatriyas are our armed forces who protect our borders, but we need Kshatriyas and Kshatriya blood to even set our narrative right when people try to convert us or belittle our identity deliberately. So, if we keep silent when adharma is happening, we become a part of it. So, Sanatana Dharma is not just about ahimsa (while Ahimsa is the ideal in a perfect world), but it is a phenomenal guide and universal laws on many things including situational leadership and speaking up and acting to protect Dharma even when everyone else is silent due to their fear / self-interest.

So just to know our history, and ensure our future generations know our history I will be writing about some of the most barbaric of Invaders, so we never forget and never allow something like that to repeat, by staying united as Hindus for a civilizational cause:

Aurangzeb's Atrocities

Aurangzeb the Mughal Emperor who ruled over 15 crore Indians between 1658-1707 had an open hatred towards Hindus and wished to convert or kill them. First, he introduced the Jizya tax on Hindus who he considered Kafirs -lesser mortals or infidels. Based on a survey, he divided Hindus into rich, poor and middle class to calculate the quantum of tax. If people wanted to avoid the tax they had to convert to Islam. Many Hindus who couldn't pay converted to Islam to avoid financial ruin. It was the great Chatrapati Shivaji Maharaj who wrote a letter to Aurangzeb condemning this tax as one which was used to enrich Aurangzeb's empire by robbing poor Hindus. In fact, the city of Aurangabad was originally called Khadgi. Aurangzeb renamed the city to Aurangabad, and it is shameful that only in 2023 was it rightly renamed to Chatrapati Sambhajinagar. Aurangzeb also built the Shahi-Eidgah Mosque during his rule, which is adjacent to Shri Krishna Janmabhoomi over a Hindu temple. He also changed the city's name to Islamabad.

It was Aurangzeb who razed the Kashi Vishweshwar temple in 1669 and built the Gyanvapi mosque using the same foundations and materials. James Prinsep, a British numismatist, and archaeologist, had made significant contributions in recording India's history. Aurangzeb also destroyed the Somnath temple again in 1706, which had been reconstructed after Mohammad of Gazni brought it down in 1026 AD. Like this several Hindu temples in Karnataka, Orissa and Rajasthan were destroyed by Aurangzeb. Aurangzeb was brutal in the murder and rape of Hindu women. He also did not spare people of other religions. Guru Tegh Bahadur revered by the Sikhs as the 9th Nanak of 10 Gurus, was publicly beheaded in 1675 by Aurangzeb. It is sad to note that this man has several followers and admirers even today in India. Our history books that children learn from do not state the brutal facts about our Invaders and praise their magnanimity, leadership and culture. We must ensure our children know the sacrifices of their people and how lucky they are to live in a free India today and must never take their freedom for granted as divisive forces still exist within our own land.

Tipu Sultan

Tipu Sultan is often hailed for fighting against the British. But do you know that this man was the reason for the rape of over 800+ Melkote Iyengar women and subsequent brutal murder of Iyengar men, women and children on a Deepavali day in the 1790s? Till today these Iyengars do not celebrate Diwali because of this tragedy. Tipu Sultan hailed as a benevolent ruler, circumcised Hindu and Christian men and forced Hindus to eat beef. It is important that our children understand this religious bigotry exists so they can protect themselves in future if it were to repeat as we do not have hatred towards any religion as per Sanatana Dharma. This does not mean we do not have the right to protect ourselves if attacked for being Hindus ever again by any destructive force.

The British:

No colonizer has been as evil as the British were to their colonies. Not only did the East India company milk India of its natural resources and riches, but the British were also responsible for making us subservient. The British hit our Vedic education system and made the English language aspirational. The British created an intellectual caste – those who could speak and read English and those who couldn't. The British understood that India could not be destabilized unless its education system was changed, and the native Indians developed an inferiority complex. As Mahaperiyava points out, many Brahmins took the bait and developed a deep inferiority complex about their Vedic origins and rituals and shunned them all together to become 'progressive' English speaking 'intellectuals'. The British and Winston Churchill were responsible for the Bengal Famine of 1943 during World War II that killed 3 million people. How did this happen? In 1942 the Japanese took control of Myanmar from the British. The British destroyed everything in Bengal including food and farms to prevent the Japanese from entering Bengal. Winston Churchill didn't bother about the plight of the poor Bengalis who couldn't afford the extremely high price which went from Rs. 2 to Rs. 40

per KG. There were dead bodies all over the streets and people didn't even have the energy to perform last rites for their dead family members. People started migrating to towns begging for food, but nobody had enough food to share with anyone. Yasmin Khan a researcher in Oxford University writes about the British 'denial policy' – she writes "The idea was that things would be razed to the ground, including crops, and also the boats that could transport the crops. So that when the Japanese came, they wouldn't have resources to expand their invasion. The impact of the denial policy on the famine is well evidenced." To make things worse the grains from Bengal were exported to Europe to feed the soldiers fighting World War 2 and denying Indians of their own food.

The British treated us as second-class citizens and slaves in our own land. They jailed freedom fighters like Veer Savarkar in the cellular jail in Port Blair and tortured them in the most inhuman ways possible. It is because of the great sacrifices of freedom fighters like Mahatma Gandhi, Subash Chandra Bose, Bal Gangadhar Thilak, Chandrashekar Azad, Veer Savarkar, Sardar Vallabhai Patel, thousands of other freedom fighters and lakhs of common people who lost their lives or struggled, we are free today from the clutches of the worst period of British Colonial rule.

CHAPTER 24

ARE WE AGAINST OTHER RELIGIONS? UNITY OF RELIGIONS

As I have said from the very beginning of my book, a true practitioner of Hinduism can never be against any religion. Sanatana Dharma is arguably the only religion in the world that unequivocally accepts all religions as true if followed in peace without harming others or converting people by force or coercion. As Mahaperiyava says, all religions have one common ideal, worship of the Lord, and all of them proclaim that there is but one God. Bhakti or devotion to the One God is same in all religions. This one God accepts your devotion irrespective of the manner of your worship, whether it is according to this or that religion. So, he goes on to say that there is no need to abandon the religion of your birth and embrace another. Do you see that world peace can be achieved only through this all-embracing thought of Sanatana Dharma where we accept people of all faiths and their practices without foisting our way and ideologies on them? If only people understood this instead of hating one another, the world would be a much better place.

So, whether one goes to a temple, church, mosque or Gurudwara, or doesn't go anywhere and prays at home, he or she will realize the one and only Paramatma, Allah, Jesus, Buddha or whatever name you wish to give the one God! While the rituals and symbols may be different, I do not understand why it is so hard for people to understand that they are merely fighting over dominance of their God over another person's God when the One God is within us no matter what name you give him or her?? It is sometimes baffling to me that such a simple concept if understood will stop all bigotry and need for religious conversions. Religions were born based on the disposition and spiritual maturity of people in a particular time and place, but all religions say that there is one true God. So many wars have been fought based on what you call that one true God! We are mad, because who cares what you call that God right? As Mahaperiyava says, "converts demean not only the religion of their birth but also the one to which they convert. Indeed, they do demean God.

From here I wish to quote Mahaperiyava, as he so succinctly and beautifully talks about the Unity of Religions in the book Hindu Dharma:

Quoting an excerpt straight from Chapter 6 on Unity of Religions of Hindu Dharma by HH Jagadguru Chdrashekarendra Sarasvati Swamigal:

"A man leaves the religion of his birth because he thinks there is something wanting in it," so you may think. "Why does the Svamigal say then that the convert demeans the new religion that he embraces?". I will tell you why. Is not because they think God is not the same in all religions that people embrace a new faith? By doing so, they see God in a reduced form, don't they? They presumably believe that the God of the religion of their birth is useless and jump to another faith. But do they believe that the God of their new religion is a universal Lord? No. No. If they did there would no need for any change of faith. Why do people embrace a new faith? Is it not because they believe continuance in the religion of their birth would mean denial of the God of the new faith to which they are attracted? This means that they place limitations on their new religion as well as on its God. When they convert to a new religion, apparently out of respect for it, they indeed dishonour it. <Confusing? Read it again and again and again. As these are pearls of wisdom from a Mahaan that this divided world needs to hear again and again. I will add- If one moves from one faith to another thinking that religion only has a true God, does it not mean that there is more than one God, when there is but one God?>

One big difference between Hinduism and other faiths is that it does not proclaim that it alone shows the path to liberation. Our Vedic religion alone has not practiced conversion and the reason for it is that our forefathers were well aware that all religions are nothing but different paths to realise the one and only Paramatman, The Vedas proclaim, "The wise speak of the One Truth by different names." (Ekam Sat Viprah Bahudha Vadanti – The truth is One, but the paths are many). Sri Krishna says in the Gita "In whatever name or form a man worships me, I increase his faith and make him firm and steady in that worship*"

"Ye Yathaa Maam prpadyante Taamstathaiva bhajaamyaham Mama Vartmaa'nuvartante manusyaah Paartha sarvasah" Bhagavad Gita 4.11

And says one of the Azhvars "Avaravar tamatamadu tarivari vahaivahai avaravar iraiyavar" i.e. How a man prays depends on the level of his understanding of the Lord

This is the reason why Hindus have not practiced – like adherents of other religions – proselytization and religious persecution. Nor have they waged anything like crusades or jihads.

Our long history is sufficient proof of this. All historians accept the fact of our religious tolerance. They observe that, when an empire like Srivijaya (The empire comprising Sumatra and some other islands in Indonesia, that flourished for several centuries attaining its peak of glory in 7th century AD) was established in the East, people accepted our culture and our way of life willingly, not because they were imposed on them by force. They further remark that Hinduism spread through trade and not through force.

In my opinion the Vedic religion was once prevalent all over the world. Certain ruins and relics found in various regions of the planet attest to this fact. Even historians who disagree with my view concede that in the past people in many lands accepted Indian culture and the Indian way of life and not on account of any force on our part,

When a passenger arrives in a station by train he is besieged by the driver of the horse cart, by the rikshawala, by the cabbie, and so on. He hires the vehicle in which he like to be driven to his destination. It cannot be said with reason that those who ply the different vehicles are guilty of competing with one another for the fare. After all it is their livelihood. But it makes no sense for the adherents of various faiths to vie with one another to take a man to the one and only destination that is God.

There is a bridge across a river, consisting of a number of arches, each of them built to the same design and measurement. To the man sitting next to a particular arch it would appear to be bigger than the other arches. So is the case with people belonging to a particular religion. They feel that their religion alone is great and want others to embrace it. There is in fact no such need for anyone to leave the religion of his birth for another.

That the beliefs and customs of the various religions are different cannot be a cause for complaint. Nor is there any need to make all of them similar. The important thing is for the followers of the various

faiths to live in harmony with one another. The goal must be unity, not uniformity."

*End of quote from Mahaperiyava's Hindu Dharma

If all people of the world read the above pearls of wisdom from the Jagadguru and internalize it, there would be world peace! Such is his clarity, grace and knowledge about Sanatana Dharma and all religions and their unity! We need to educate more and more people of all faiths about this to end unnecessary wars over religion!

At this juncture, India has countless stories of the Lord appearing in the form in which one worships Him/Her, yes, Her (Though Paramatma is formless and genderless) and here is one such touching story from Madurai:

Peter Padam Madurai Meenakshi Temple

A British Collector named Rous Peter was appointed as Collector of Madurai from 1812 to 1828.

Though a Christian by faith, he respected all faiths including Hinduism and also honoured local practices.

Collector Peter was the temple administrator of the Meenakshi Amman Temple and conducted all his duties with sincerity and honesty and respected the religious sentiments of all people and treated people of all faiths equally.

This noble trait earned him the popular nickname 'Peter Pandian'.

Goddess Meenakshi Amman Temple was situated between Collector Peter's residence and office.

Every day he used to go to the office by his horse and while crossing the temple, he used to get down from his horse, remove his hat and his shoes and crossed the whole path bare foot.

Through this small gesture he expressed his reverence to the Goddess!

One day there was a heavy downpour in Madurai city and River Vaigai was in spate.

The Collector was sleeping in his residence and was suddenly disturbed and woken up by the sound of anklets and he got out of bed to find out where the sound had come from.

He saw a small girl wearing pattuvastrams (silk garments) and precious ornaments and addressing him, 'Peter, come this way.'

And he came out to follow her and was running behind the little girl to find out who she was !

As he came out of the house and was running, he was shocked as he turned to see behind him, his residence (the whole bungalow) being washed away by the flood waters of River Vaigai!

He turned to follow the girl, but she disappeared in thin air!

He saw that the girl ran without any shoes and was wearing anklets.

He believed that his devotion for Mother Goddess Meenakshi had saved his life.

Later, he wished to give a gift to Lord Meenakshi Amman & consulted the priest of the temple and ordered for a pair of golden shoes (padukas) for Goddess Meenakshi Amman since he had seen the little girl with bare feet.

It is thus that the pair of Paadhukams consist of:

- 412 rubies,
- 72 emeralds, and
- 80 diamonds

were made and donated to the temple.

His name Peter was sculpted on the padukas.

Till this day the pair of Paadhukams are known as 'Peter Paadhukam'.

When Rous Peter retired from service, he refused to go back to England and settled in Madurai.

He also wished that when he died, he should be buried in a position such that his eyes faced the temple.

It is interesting to note that in that graveyard, Rous Peter's grave is positioned the way he wished whereas all the other graves face the other way.

To this day, every year at the time of 'Chitrai (Chaitra) Festival', utsava moorthy of Goddess Meenakshi Amman is decorated with these Peter Padukams.

This incident happened more than 200 years back in 1818.

Till this day, once every year one of the descendants of Rous Peter visits the temple.

This was a good Britisher who respected our Dharma, and Goddess Meenakshi literally saved his life. So, the beauty of Sanatana Dharma transcends religious beliefs because Dharma is universal and timeless.

CHAPTER 25

IS MASTURBATION BAD?

This is a question almost all of us have asked ourselves as teenagers when our Kama (lust/desire) increases due to hormonal changes. I am addressing this here as I wish someone had talked to me about this when I needed answers as a teenager (This should not be a taboo subject as Sanatana Dharma understands the basic carnal desires -Kama that happens during puberty). I am writing this for my son and daughter and for every teenager anywhere in the world so they can make informed decisions about their sexuality. I asked myself this question many years after my teenage years also and I experientially understood it. When I started doing my Sandhya Vandhanam and Nadi Sothanam Pranayama (Alternatively breathing in through the left nostril, holding the breath and breathing out through the right nostril and vice versa right to left, slowly 10 times before the Gayatri Japam), again when I was 29 years old, I realized that my compulsive urges reduced. I then delved into reading about why celibacy is an important aspect of yogic science. My practice started increasing my focus, clarity and intuition despite having missed doing it during the crucial teenage years. Imagine how powerful it would have been if I had been taught the correct way to do the pranayama when I had my thread ceremony? It is sad that many priests don't teach you the Pranayama techniques properly, as that is crucial and has a major positive impact on one's emotional, mental, physical and spiritual wellbeing.

So, during Brahmacharya in the Gurukul times, the student would be taught various yogic techniques and the Vedas to focus his mind and not succumb to desires. So, what essentially happens is, Semen which contains sperms and life force (Prana) gets channelized and becomes a subtle energy form that travels up your spine to the back of your head. This energy is called Ojas. So, without being moralistic and saying whether masturbation is good or bad, we must understand that there are huge benefits to not wasting one's semen which has the capacity to bring to the world a new life, through masturbation. This is the reason celibate Gurus have a Tejas or aura around them and many have otherworldly powers. Brahmacharya gives the student the necessary mental and physical strength to absorb the Vedas and even all things that modern education has to offer with clarity and without getting distracted. Mind you, these yogic techniques do not suppress or diminish one's sex drive, they merely remove the animal compulsion for sex, which is the most powerful force of nature, and help you use it when needed. Even animals have a time and place to mate but we humans supposedly with a sixth sense have lost the ability to channelize this and this is affecting our teenagers' mental and physical health adversely. Today with the free rampant availability of pornography and even casual sex partners, we have to try our best to tell our children that there is a time and place for everything in Sanatana Dharma – nothing is Taboo, and everything that is in our Sastras is scientific and for our well-being. We can produce the brightest, most intuitive, dharmic children on planet Earth if we delve deep into our spiritual core and yogic science. So, my request to you if you are a parent and don't feel comfortable talking to your 14–18-year-old son or daughter about this, please ask them to read this book. So, is it ok for girls to masturbate as they don't release semen? The simple answer is that during orgasm the entire nervous system consumes tremendous amounts of energy. Our body is an energy superstructure. So, whether for men or women masturbation is best avoided or moderated as marriages are getting inordinately delayed these days. A simple way would be to analyse your mental clarity, focus and energy levels immediately after masturbation and the same after abstinence for a few weeks. Do not suppress the urge as it is futile, but learn yogic techniques like Nadi Sothanam Pranayama from a trained yoga practitioner / Guru and then explore abstinence. The best way to understand is through experience, as no amount of lectures can help you when your hormones are on overdrive as a teenager especially.

While I am not dedicating a chapter to this, I would like to highlight that alcohol has become a social norm today, at least in the big cities. This was not the case even 20 years back in India. Again, I make no judgement of people who drink or not, but the habit-forming capacity of alcohol is best avoided for those on the spiritual path as is anything that becomes compulsive in nature. Similarly for drugs and smoking which can drag one down physically and mentally. We need to safeguard our youngsters from blindly aping the western world as today many from the west have done these things to death, not found fulfilment and are now coming to India to soul search through Yoga, meditation and spirituality and lead a peaceful life.

CHAPTER 26

WHERE ARE THE KSHATRIYAS? WHAT IS KSHATRIYA DHARMA

Kshatriya Dharma refers to the duties of one of the four Varnas viz. Brahmana, Kshatriya, Vaishya and Shudra. In the Purusha Sukta of the Rigveda, there is reference to the four Varnas. It is described there that the Kshatriyas came out of the arms of the Lord, the Creator. According to the Bhagavad Gita, Guna (quality) and Karma (kind of work) determine the Varna of a man. Shri Lord Krishna says,

"The four varnas emanated by Me, by the different distribution of qualities and actions. Know Me to be the author of them, though the actionless and inexhaustible" (Ch. IV-13).

These qualities or Gunas are three in number viz., Sattva (purity), Rajas (passion) and Tamas (inertia) and are found in man in varying proportions. Those in whom Rajas is predominant, they are Kshatriyas. They are warriors or men of action. They fight with the enemies or invaders and defend the country. Broadly speaking, a Rajasic man with heroic quality is a Kshatriya. The underlying principle in Varna Dharma, is division of labour. The work of political administration and defence was given to the Kshatriyas.

Kshatriya-s

Shauryam, tejah, dhrutihi, dākshyam yuddhe cha api apalāyanam

Dānam, ishvaryabhāvah cha kshātram karma svabhāvjam

Kshatriyas are brave, (have) powerful personality, (can) make firm decisions, (have) ability to fight in war, (do) not withdraw from battlefield, generous, and of royal behaviour - Bhagavad Gitā, XVIII.43

Kshatriyas were physically strong, well trained in the art of warfare, and use of weapons. One of them would become the king. In the days of king Bharat, the ruler was selected on the basis of his knowledge and capabilities. The king's primary responsibility was to protect the population, provide for necessities of life like food, water, schools, roads, etc. Other Kshatriyas would be in the army.

To know the ideal Kshatriya one has to study Lord Ram and the Ramayana. Lord Rama was the epitome of Dharma and was a true Kshatriya. A kshatriya is one who fights to protect Dharma and his people. He is not a war monger like an Asura but has sattva guna and the rajas guna when needed to fight and defend dharma. A Kshatriya too has the thread ceremony and was well-versed in the Vedas, but many Kshatriyas today do not have the thread ceremony. So Kshatriyas could learn the Vedas but not teach it as their primary Dharma was to be warriors and safeguard Kingdoms, their people and land/ country. As Lord Krishna tells Arjuna (A Kshatriya) in the Bhagavad Gita, it is a duty of a Kshatriya to fight adharma even if it means one has to fight against his own elders and brothers. When Arjuna goes weak in the knees and has severe anxiety and doubts, Lord Krishna tells him that he must not think he is killing his relatives but he is protecting Dharma for the well-being of the world. In today's world when our Army performs counter-terrorism operations, there are people who talk about human rights for terrorists. This is the weakness that modern day Kshatriyas have to oppose. Terrorists kill innocent civilians and it is the duty of our Army to protect us. In the modern world we need Kshatriya blood more than ever. Kshatriyas have to be leaders in setting narratives to protect the ever-eroding faith in our Dharma amongst people. They should be brave to speak out and lead the way in talking about the greatness of our religion. Kshatriyas would do great in serving our great country in the armed forces. While today's armed forces have people from various religions and castes, hereditary Kshatriyas like the descendants of Marathas will still have it in their blood and have the strength and courage to protect our most vulnerable people in the face of war. Today we have to win the battle of ideology and narrative. In today's world in the Kaliyugam we have many Adharmic forces and we need Kshatriyas to be brave and speak about the importance of Dharma to set our grand narrative as our country. Kshatriya dharma is as much about narrative as it is in fighting on the battlefield when the need arises, to protect our country and innocent people of the world, against asuric forces. It is a shame what happened to Kashmiri pundits in 1990. Where were the Kshatriyas? Till today more than 3 lakh Kashmiri Pundits are fearful to go back to their homes in J&K for the fear of religious persecution. When a Kashmiri Pundit couple came to see my Guru (HH Jagadguru Vijayendra Saraswati Swamigal) and told him that they fear going back to Kashmir even after article 370 has been revoked, he told them to go bravely. We need the Kshatriyas to protect these Brahmins when they go back. Things are changing now in Kashmir and I hope all the Kashmiri pundits can be resettled soon.

Kshatriyas in the modern world should try to learn the Vedas from a learned Guru, do their rites for their departed ancestors and always speak for and work for Dharmic causes that would protect innocent people of all walks of life and faiths.

I will leave you with an interesting translation of a passage from the Mahabharata that I read about Kshatriyas and their importance

Kshatriyas were created from the arms of the creator. Hence, they pride on their physical strength.

The Agni Purana also mentions Protection and suppression of the wicked as special (duties enjoined) on a kshatriya.

The main job of a kshatriya is fighting to protect the प्रजा || prajas (creatures of his land) and defend his

क्षेत्र || kshetra (land), because that is his natural inclination and the best use of his qualities, as Krishna has stated specifically :

स्वधर्ममपि चावेक्ष्य न विकम्पितुमर्हसि ।
धर्म्याद्धि युद्धाच्छ्रेयोऽन्यत्क्षत्रियस्य न विद्यते ॥२.३१॥

यदृच्छया चोपपन्नं स्वर्गद्वारमपावृतम् ।
सुखिनः क्षत्रियाः पार्थ लभन्ते युद्धमीदृशम् ॥२.३२॥ **Bhagavad Gita**

sva dharmam api caveksya na vikampitum arhasi |
dharmyad hi yuddhac chreyo 'nyat ksatriyasya na vidyate || (Bhagvadgita 2.31)

yadricchaya copapannam svarga dvaram apavritam |
sukhinah ksatriyah partha labhante yuddham idrisam || (Bhagvadgita 2.32)

Meaning : Considering your own dharmic duty you should not hesitate, because for a kshatriya there is nothing better than fighting a dharmic battle. O Arjuna, happy are the kshatriyas to whom such opportunity comes unsought. For a warrior, engaging in such a battle is like having the doors of heaven open in front of him.

However, the warrior spirit of a kshatriya is not the war mongering, blood lust, and cruelty of the asuras; he is not a brawling bully and he avoids confrontation and conflict if there is any other option still possible, as the Pandavas demonstrated in practice in their dealings with the aggressive Duryodhana and his brothers.

A person who has a kshatriya nature is influenced by सत्त्व गुण || sattva guna with a latent tendency to

रजस् गुण || rajas guna, and therefore he needs to be trained more strictly to a harder discipline. His natural qualities of heroism, leadership, resourcefulness and generosity are sattvic, but if rajas is not controlled, they can turn into arrogance and thirst for power over people and wealth, deceitfulness, and manipulation of others through corruption and dirty politics. Therefore, the Guru trains the kshatriya students in overcoming selfishness and egotism, through the study of the transcendental science as well as in sacrificing one's life in defence of the prajas. The activities or duties of the kshatriya, determined by his particular nature, are heroism, charisma, determination, resourcefulness, steadiness in battle, charity and sense of leadership.

Kshatriyas are educated and trained in strategy and diplomacy in dealing with the enemy – the first attempt is sama, treating the opponent like a friend and allowing sufficient space for his livelihood and prosperity, the second is dana, trying to win them with peace offerings and gifts, the third attempt is bheda, trying to break up hostile alliances and facing one enemy at the time, and only as a last resort one should resort to danda, punishment as in taking physical action against the offender.

A true Kshatriya is always on the front line, before anybody else, in the thick of the battle, and is the best example to follow. He works harder and longer hours than anyone else, and is ever ready (24 hours a day, 7 days a week) to sacrifice his own sense gratification, comforts, possessions, position and personal life (by living and by dying) for the sake of the kingdom and the prajas – whether the kingdom is a large country or a village, a neighbourhood or any group of people who look up to him for guidance. A true Kshatriya takes responsibility not only for his own failures but also for collective defeats, inspires and encourages others and helps them to rise and progress to become qualified leaders in turn. He demonstrates concern, care and affection for the prajas just like a good father behaves with his children, engages them happily and appropriately, and always watches over their well-being, over and above his own immediate family and relatives.

There is a specific code of conduct for kshatriyas; non-combatants should never be attacked or harmed, and property that is not directly connected to the fighting should not be destroyed; for example, the encampments where the warriors retire for the night are not to be touched. Even on the battlefield a warring enemy should not be attacked if he is unprepared, unarmed, distracted, distraught, or if he admits defeat.

My observation: See the beauty of Dharma even in war? Today most of these things are not followed and even women and children are being killed! People's (civilian) homes are being destroyed and people are fighting over whose God is superior, when there is only one God! Thankfully the Indian Army is still one of the most Dharmic Armies in the world and never attacks anyone for land or power and only attacks when attacked, for purposes of defence and offensive

defence in case of terror attacks, to neutralize terror camps. Bharath should always adopt dharma even in case of war and protect the vulnerable. Kshatriya dharma is very important in these cases.

Enumerating the importance of kshatriyas in the society, the Mahabharata says,

यदि निःक्षत्रियो लोको जगत्स्यादधरोत्तरम्॥ 13.208.21

रक्षणात्क्षत्रियैरेव जगद्भवति शाश्वतम्। 13.208.22

If there were no kshatriyas in this world, then there would have been great chaos in the world. The world is sustained by the protection of the kshatriyas.

A Few Key Things Kshatriyas Can Do to Protect Dharma:

1. Support all dharmic causes and live in Bharath if you can. If you live abroad be a cheerleader from wherever you live.
2. Protect the Bharatiya narrative with your life and soul. NEVER SPEAK ILL ABOUT OUR RELIGION. Do not allow anyone to speak ill of our religion and Dharma.
3. Perform the thread ceremony for your sons and make sure the father and son do the Sandhyavandhanam and Gayatri Mantra thrice a day. Make your children learn the Vedas and recite them.
4. Teach your daughters simple pujas that they can do daily like offering food to God, birds